Home Decorating

Home Decorating

GUILD OF
MASTER CRAFTSMAN
PUBLICATIONS

Jeannine McAndrew

First published 2008 by
Guild of Master Craftsman Publications Ltd.
Castle Place, 166 High Street, Lewes, East Sussex BN7 1XU

Text © Jeannine McAndrew 2008
© in the Work GMC Publications Ltd

ISBN 978-1-86108-622-8

A catalogue record for this book is available from the British Library.

Associate Publisher Jonathan Bailey
Production Manager Jim Bulley
Managing Editor Gerrie Purcell
Project Editor Gill Parris
Managing Art Editor Gilda Pacitti
Designer Chloë Alexander
Picture Research Hedda Roennevig

Set in Clarendon and Meta Plus
Colour origination by GMC Reprographics
Printed and bound in Thailand by Kyodo Nation Printing

Contents

Planning

Preparation

Paints and Painting

Using Wallpaper

4

5

Interior Updates

Introduction

USING COLOUR
If you choose your colours carefully, simply painting the walls can transform a room (*above*). Even if you keep to a relatively neutral palette, the way you choose to decorate your home allows you to express your personality (*right*).

It seems that we are obsessed with decorating, watching numerous television programmes on the subject and reading many books. And with good reason: if you own your home, making it look appealing is a great way to add value to what is, after all, your biggest asset.

And, if you're renting at the moment, there are still lots of simple ways you can add a personal touch, even if you don't want to invest a lot of time and money making drastic changes.

Decorating is about expressing your individual style and making a place feel like home. There are few tasks that offer such instant results – if you simply spend a day or two painting a room, you can literally transform it.

The choice of colours you use can make an area seem bigger, lighter, cosier, more dramatic or more intimate. Your choice of wallpaper, colours, paints and applications will all combine to make a personal statement about your home and how you want to live in it.

There is often a fair amount of trial and error when it comes to choosing colour schemes so, to avoid costly mistakes when deciding how to decorate your home, it really pays to do your research first.

Think about each room you plan to work on and how you are likely to use it. Simple factors – such as the time of day you will tend to use the room – can have a huge impact on the kind of light you are likely to see it in, and the most suitable colours to set it off to best advantage. For example, rich colours such as deep red are often used in dining rooms, and they look wonderful at night enhanced by candlelight. But if you also plan to have breakfast in that room every day, you may want something less dramatic to look at over your cornflakes before you go to work!

It is also helpful to consider the year-round use of each area of your home. Calming shades of blue might make a conservatory even more inviting on a hot summer's day, but on a chilly winter's evening, will a cool colour scheme put you off using the room?

Finally, it is well worth considering your individual circumstances. If you intend to stay in your current home for many years, you can really go to town and experiment with decorating schemes that are all about exploring your own personal taste, and the various interests of your family.

If you are planning to move in the next year or two, then it is perhaps wise to be rather more conservative, and opt for a palette of neutral shades that will appeal to the widest possible audience when you come to show potential buyers around your home.

Even then, furniture and accessories can be more flamboyant – whether in colour or style – if that is your preference, and add a lively touch to an otherwise neutral room.

THINK IT THROUGH
Simple schemes can be very effective, and white walls, a white painted floor and neutral acccessories make for a very inviting bathroom (*above left*). The inspiration for your decorating scheme can come from a diverse range of sources, and might even stem from a particular piece of furniture (*above*). Flowers and plants enhance the home and will always add a welcome splash of colour to a room (*left*).

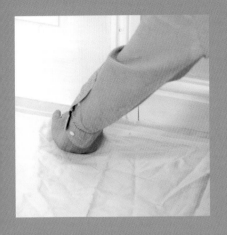

1

Planning

Time spent researching the many options

available will be invaluable, and ensure that

you are happy in your newly decorated home.

Researching Your Style

Decorating your home offers a unique opportunity to develop your own look. Treasured furniture and accessories might determine the look you want, but also consider other rooms and homes you like, and why. If you feel inspired, the whole process of decorating is considerably more enjoyable, so take time out to create a solid idea of how you want the room to look. Books are a wealth of information, but pick up magazines and brochures, too. You can cut pages of rooms that you like from magazines and start putting them together in a folder. Visit your local DIY store and pick up paint charts, catalogues and any other information they have and you'll soon start developing a sense of the styles that you like. By talking it over with a friend or partner, you'll be able to pinpoint exactly what appeals to you about different looks and colours.

Interior designers often create a 'mood board' before they decorate a room. This is a surprisingly simple technique that can really help you to clarify the aspects of the look you want to achieve. All you need is a large piece of cardboard (an old cereal packet will do), a stapler and the pictures, paint charts and other images you've amassed. You can then add scraps of fabrics and even ideas of flooring materials to get an overview of how the room could come together.

If you are undecided, make up a few mood boards. Take your time over this, because any work you do at this stage won't be wasted. For example, a colour scheme that you reject for a sunny bedroom, might prove ideal for a dark bathroom at the back of the house. Your mood boards will help you to decide what your likes and dislikes are before you've spent time and money painting. The following pages cover some of the different themes that are popular at the moment. It is not an exhaustive list, but it may provide the starting point for you to develop your own ideas.

PLAN AHEAD

You may have treasured possessions which will influence your style, but it's well worth doing research, too: books on interior decorating, cut-outs from magazines, brochures, paint charts and mood boards with samples of paint and fabric will all help you to achieve a truly memorable room.

AN AIRY FEEL
Simple, unfitted
furniture and a
tiled floor create a
wonderfully relaxed
area in this spacious
country kitchen (*below*).

Country

Whether you have a little cottage, a
Victorian terrace, or a modern flat, there
are elements of country style that can look
great in a bedroom, living room or kitchen.
This is a fresh, summery look that can help
you to feel relaxed and comfortable the
minute you step into the room.

Country style is particularly suitable
for rooms that connect the inside with
the exterior of your home, so it may be
worth considering for a conservatory,
or indeed any room that has French
doors or large windows that look out
onto the garden.

Colours

Light, feminine shades are ideal – many country homes in Britain have small rooms with little windows, so the interior decor needs to be light and fresh.

Wallpapers

Look out for designs with a subtle background, for example cream highlighted with muted blues and pinks, with natural motifs, such as flowers or fruit.

Fabrics and Accessories

Country style is eclectic, people traditionally tended to make do and mend, so look out for items such as patchwork quilts, rag rugs, plain muslin curtains, sprigged florals and linen, edged with lace, which are perfect for a country-style room.

FRESH AND PRETTY
Painted furniture, fresh flowers and light and pretty fabrics give a country feel to a room.

Contemporary/Urban

Often considered to be quite a masculine style, the contemporary or urban look is ideal in loft apartments or any rooms that house audiovisual items such as a computer, television, or music system. Modern, bold and often edgy, you can opt for strong contrasts such as grey walls, red leather sofas and black soft furnishings for example. This look is also ideal in kitchens, bathrooms and wet rooms that are utilitarian and designed to be streamlined and easy to use and keep clean and tidy.

BOLD AND EDGY
Contrast shapes, colours and textures to create an eye-catching modern look (*below*).

Colours

This look is all about making a statement, so restrict your palette to mainly neutrals like white, black and grey and accentuate it with bold swathes of colour, such as a red stripe across a grey wall for example.

Wallpapers

These should be either neutral if used on all the walls, or a more dramatic design if used sparingly.

Fabric and Accessories

Opt for natural fibres in neutral shades with an interesting textural appeal. Avoid trims and decoration, choose blinds rather than curtains, and keep the look simple and uncluttered.

MAKE A STATEMENT
Use dramatic colours
on your walls as the
perfect backdrop for
stylish items such as
leather seating and
perspex furniture (*left*).

WARM AND HOMELY
Inspired by the best
of 1950s style, the
vintage look is ideal
for kitchens (*below*).

Vintage Chic

Homely and welcoming but effortlessly stylish, this look is understandably popular for kitchens, utility rooms and, in fact, anywhere that the family might relax. This feminine style is characterized by classic floral fabrics and ticking stripes in rose-pink and forget-me-not blue. Equally at home in a rural or city setting, this look is designed to help you enjoy the time you spend at home, whether you're getting on with the laundry, baking a cake, or having a garden party with plenty of bunting.

Colours

Pale pastel shades, or bright, fresh colours are ideal.

Wallpapers

Used sparingly, bold floral designs, dots and stripes really bring this look to life.

Fabrics and Accessories

Choose embroidered bed linen, tea-towels and cushion covers, with details such as tiny flowers or overblown roses. You can mix and match, because the subtle backdrop of pale shades gives a few bold touches the room that they need to breathe.

USE SOFT COLOURS
A mixture of pale pastel colours can create a restful environment (*below*).

Painting the floor is a fast and inexpensive way to transform a room. Specialist paint in many colours is available from DIY stores.

TIMELESS ELEGANCE
Elegant and understated, checked cushions and white furniture create a light, airy room (*above*).

Gustavian/Classical

This Swedish style has timeless appeal. Minimal without being cold, this look works well in large or small rooms, as it is based on lots of creamy white and very pale shades of blue, grey and pink. White-painted wooden floorboards and furniture are enlivened with touches of gingham or toile de jouy, to create an elegant, inviting home.

LESS IS MORE
This style is simple,
uncluttered and
understated, making it
ideal for rooms that
aren't in constant use.

Colours

Choose the softest pastels in blue, pink
and dove grey, with perhaps a touch of
apple green.

Wallpapers

King Gustav of Sweden made this style
popular in the eighteenth century. Then,
even wealthier homes could not afford the
expensive wallpapers that he had so admired
in the palace of Louis XVI, so painted murals
were seen on walls instead. Fortunately,
wallpaper is now more affordable.

Fabrics and Accessories

Gingham, toiles, simple blinds in
subtle shades and classic white or pale
embroidered white fabrics are ideal.

MIX AND MATCH
Accentuate original
details such as
skirting boards and
dado rails by painting
them in a contrasting
colour (*below*).

Period Drama

If you are lucky enough to own a period home, there are a number of good reasons for choosing to decorate it in the style that would have been in vogue when it was designed. Older properties were built with great attention to detail and often include original features such as fireplaces, skirting boards, dado rails and architectural mouldings that add character and value to the property. Historically accurate colours and styles can help to emphasize these features, enabling you to create a home that has immediate impact and a unified appeal.

toptip*

Many of the leading
paint companies
offer specific colour
charts for the
different periods,
so you don't need
to be an expert on
history to get the
look right if you
own an older home.

GET THE LOOK
A rolltop bath (*far left*)
Victorian tiles in a
fireplace (*left*) a
strategically placed
desk (*below left*), or
carefully chosen
wallpaper (*below*), all
help achieve the effect.

Georgian

This period marks one of the most stylish and graceful eras in architecture, and homes built in the eighteenth century often have tall ceilings, large windows and light, airy interiors. The palette used at the time featured classic colours associated with stone, marble and alabaster. The shades used in interiors tended to be subtle and understated, while exteriors often featured strong blues and greens, which were popular on doors, gates and railings.

Colours

Muted, classic and elegant shades of lavender grey, ash violet, pale sienna and pea green were favoured.

Wallpapers

Due to their expensive nature silk, paper and flock wall-coverings were only used in the homes of the most affluent people in the eighteenth century.

Fabrics and Accessories

Natural fibres such as silk, cotton and linen would have been used, in a mixture of some very simple designs and more complex, exotic motifs, as influences from around the world became more fashionable.

CLASSIC STYLE
Green Verditer is a versatile shade that was very popular in the 1700s (*facing page*). Neutral shades and natural fibres give a timeless look (*above*). Symmetry and a strong sense of proportion are key themes in Georgian homes (*right*).

Victorian

People often think that home decor during the reign of Queen Victoria was fussy, dark and stuffy. However, during the 80 years or so of this period, there were a number of both vibrant and muted styles, and you can choose from a selection of rich and attractive colours to suit your home. A three-part scheme was often employed, where different colours were used above and below the dado rail, and again between the picture rail and the ceiling. Stronger colours were deemed suitable in dining rooms and libraries, while sitting rooms and bedrooms would have featured lighter shades.

Colours

Led by famous designers such as Augustus Pugin and William Morris, this period demonstrated a fascination with mediaeval style. Colours were often rich and bold in combinations of blue, green, red and yellow.

Wallpapers

In the 1830s more affordable, roller-printed wall coverings became available, and wallpaper became extremely popular. Designs often featured plants and animals. Flock was often used in reception rooms while floral papers were usually featured in bedrooms.

Fabric and Accessories

Rich and opulent fabrics such as damask and velvet were popular, as were William Morris fabric designs, which can still be bought today. Chintz was also widely used when a lighter touch was more appropriate.

RICH AND BOLD
William Morris fabrics are still popular (*below*).

A LIGHTER TOUCH
In this innovative era, light colours such as pale green were even used in rooms such as studies (*below*).

From 1901 onwards, Edwardian style was bright, bold and innovative, in marked contrast to the clutter and dark colours of Victorian interiors. Leading up to the flamboyance of the Art Deco style, people were keen to paint their homes in bold combinations such as primrose yellow and leaf green.

Colours

Vivid hues that reflected nature were extremely popular, with more striking shades of lilac, teal and peacock blue now widely available to the general public, due to advances in the manufacturing process. Chrome became extremely fashionable, and details in woodwork were often embellished with gold or silver gilding.

Wallpapers

Designs featuring wisteria, trellis, ribbons and bows were in vogue, as were textured, raised designs such as lincrusta and anaglypta.

Fabrics and Accessories

Liberty prints became very popular and many were inspired by Japanese and Indian styles. The sinuous designs of Art Noveau were widely used.

PERFECT HARMONY
Glamorous colours and sweeping curves are ideal for Edwardian homes (*right*).

Rococo/Romantic

This look is all about exuberance and fun. Corresponding roughly with the reign of Louis XV in France (1710–74), the term gains its name from a combination of the French word for shell (*rocaille*) and the Italian word for Baroque style (*barocco*). If you want to indulge in a romantic theme – perhaps for a bedroom or a dramatic candlelit dining room – then you may want to take a tip or two from French style in the 1700s. The look is elaborately ornate, featuring whimsical sweeps and flourishes, asymmetrical curves, cupids and gilt accessories.

Colours

This is a light-hearted and optimistic style featuring dusky pinks, ivory, purple and lavender shades.

Wallpapers

Choose delicate but elaborate designs in iridescent pastel colours.

Fabrics and Accessories

Look out for opulent silks, satins and velvets in rich tones, perhaps complemented with embroidery, gold fringes and passementerie. Mirrors and pictures with ornate gilt frames will complete the look, as will a chandelier or coloured glassware.

ADD EMBELLISHMENTS
Elaborate trimmings on cushions and linen are all part of the fun (*below*).

Design and Colour

Colour Theory

It was Sir Isaac Newton who first came up with the idea of the colour wheel back in 1666, and today it is still a very useful tool for deciding which colours work well together. Newton arranged the different hues in a logical sequence, as they are seen in a rainbow, from red, orange and yellow through green and blue to indigo and violet. He found that the hues next to each other on the wheel (known as harmonizing colours) work very well together. He also found that hues opposite one another on the wheel (known as complementary colours) also work very well together, as they provide maximum contrast – a bold combination that is often seen in nature. Pigments of the **primary** colours (red, yellow and blue) can be mixed to form **secondary** colours (green, orange and purple).

For example if you mix yellow and blue paint you will get a shade of green. The more subtle colours in between the different hues are often known as **tertiary** colours.

PLAN IT OUT
You can use different shades of the same colour to build up a sophisticated room scheme (*above*).
The colour wheel is a useful tool for helping to choose how to decorate a room (*left*).

How we see colour

We tend to have an emotional response to different colours, and this is often influenced by our culture. For example, washing powder manufacturers have found that in the UK we tend to think that really brilliant white is almost bluey-white, while in some parts of Europe, greenish-white is considered to look more clean. Most people consider red to be dramatic and exciting while green is viewed as a natural and calming shade. These associations can be helpful when it comes to creating the mood of a room.

The context in which a colour is seen can also influence our perception of it. The same shade of red can look quite different against a black, white or yellow background. A grey object on a green background will appear to have a red tinge. This means that the accessories you use to finish a room after you have painted it are all-important.

Light Fantastic

Bear in mind that the amount of light shining on a colour changes our perception of it dramatically. That is why colours often seem to merge into each other and can become hard to identify in the evening, as daylight fades. If, for example, you only tend to use your bedroom either late at night or early in the morning, be aware that the quality of artificial light will affect the way the colours you have chosen will look.

There are general rules about the colours you choose to paint your walls but, because of the different ways in which we interpret colour, there will be many variable factors. If you've seen a picture of a colour you really like in this book, or in a magazine, the chances are the one used in that particular room won't look quite the same on your walls.

Collect as many paint charts, sample pots of paints, and swatches of fabrics and wallpapers as you can when choosing the colours you like, so that you can look at them in the context of the room in which you intend to use them and get a really good idea about what will work best.

COLOURFUL ADDITIONS
Light shining through glass adds a jewel-like quality to a plain shelf (*top*). Books add a decorative and colourful feature to an otherwise simple room (*above*).

LIGHT AND AIRY
Muted colours give a light and relaxing feel to a room (*above*).

TRY BEFORE YOU BUY
Colour charts are a great starting point for working out a theme (*below*).

toptip*

Use sample pots of paint to determine the exact shade that looks best in your home at the times when you are most likely to be using a particular room.

doit USE COLOUR TO YOUR ADVANTAGE

Make a Large Room Feel More Cosy
Warm, earthy shades can make a room feel more intimate. Red, orange, brown, gold and terracotta are all ideal choices for bedrooms.

Here, the pale but warm walls and matching blinds make the room seem very snug and the touches of hot, stronger colour – such as scarlet and burgundy – contribute to the cosy feel of the room

Create a Feeling of Space

Pale colours such as grey, white, green, blue and lilac lead to a roomier atmosphere. To make a small room look bigger and airier, it can also help to use a monochromatic colour scheme.

For example in a bedroom all the walls, woodwork, furnishings and accessories could be in one colour such as white. The room below is light and simple – the room is uncluttered and the pale walls and minimal furniture make the room seem larger than it actually is.

Brighten up a Dull Area

The colours we associate with sunshine have the effect of making rooms appear to be more inviting. Cream, yellow, ochre and apricot all make north-facing rooms feel more summery, and are useful for bringing a year-round feeling of warmth to rooms such as a conservatory.

If you tend to feel sluggish in the mornings, you may find that painting your bedroom in pale, sunshine colours – such as lemon and buttercup – helps you to feel more like leaping out of bed! Combined with clever lighting, the right choice of paint shade can quite literally transform a room.

Create a Stimulating Atmosphere

If you want to have a lively feel in a study, hallway or living room, choose contrasting colours from opposite ends of the colour wheel such as yellow and violet or red and green.

If this combination is more bold than your tastes, use one colour as the main shade and the complementary colour to pick out certain features. Even items such as radiators can be enhanced with specialist paints in a range of hues.

Create a Restful Atmosphere

In bedrooms, soothing colours such as soft greys, lilacs, creams and taupe can create a very restful atmosphere.

Bed linen in a selection of pale and neutral shades can be mixed and matched, and will still complement the room, even if you eventually choose a new colour scheme.

Make a Room Seem Longer

Horizontal stripes give the impression of depth in a small room – ideal for bathrooms, which are often compact. Large mirrors or mirror tiles also add the illusion of space.

Colour Creation and Matching

Most of us become attached to furnishings that we amass – whether a rug or a bedspread, a comfy sofa, or a favourite painting. There may also be fixed features in the room you are decorating that you don't want to change – floor or wall tiles in a kitchen for example – and these items can form a great starting point for your colour scheme.

When choosing a look for the whole room, the colour of your starting point needn't dominate the entire area, but you can create a unified look if you use the same shade on other details in the room.

For example, if you have a red range cooker in your kitchen, while you may not want to paint the walls red, you could create dramatic impact by having red wall tiles behind the sink and using red accessories such as a kettle, tea towels or teapot to complete the theme.

Where possible, it is worth taking a sample of the item you wish to match to the DIY stores so that you can select a similar shade. However, if you are trying to match a bulky or fixed item, taking a sample with you is not a practical option. Instead, it may be easier to use a colour chart, or piece of fabric at home to match the shade as closely as you can, and take that in to the store to help you choose a selection of sample pots. In larger stores you may be able to have the exact colour you want made up for you while you wait.

If you want to choose a colour to go with a vibrant or patterned item, such as a painting or sofa, it is often a good idea to choose one of the more muted colours in the piece, and use that shade on the walls as a backdrop against which your keynote object will stand out.

CREATE HARMONY
The orange motif in the blind has been enhanced and balanced with accessories in the room, such as the glass vase on the window sill (*right*).

COMPARE/CONTRAST

Here the pale grey walls, chairs and rug set off the red accessories very effectively (*right*). The setting itself can be a good starting point for a colour scheme and, in a room like a conservatory, fresh shades of green are a very natural choice (*bottom left*). The cool white of the bath is complemented by the restful blue of the walls and white towel (*bottom right*).

Home Decorating

Tools of the Trade

Before you begin work, you'll need to organize a basic tool kit. Many items are available to hire, and this is an option well worth considering if you are only decorating one room, or if bulky tools such as ladders are required and storage space is at a premium. However, if you have a whole house to decorate, it will generally be well worth investing in the equipment you need as, if you look after it, much of your kit will last a lifetime.

Paint Brushes

Brushes are very easy to use, and most people prefer them to rollers for painting intricate surfaces. Small 1in (2.5cm) brushes are best for painting detailed areas of woodwork, such as window frames; medium 2in (5cm) brushes are designed for cutting in, or areas such as doors, while larger brushes – 4in (10cm) and over – are best used for covering more extensive areas. Always buy the best quality brushes you can afford.

Rollers

Used in conjunction with a tray, rollers apply paint over large, flat surfaces very quickly and easily. They come in two parts: the cage, which is attached to the handle and the sleeve. The sleeve can be simply detached from the cage so that you can select different options. You can choose rough roller sleeves for textured surfaces, while smooth sleeves are better for flat surfaces and for applying paints with a sheen. You can get mini rollers for painting smaller areas, but most people find that rollers are not suitable for very accurate work, so you will still need a small brush for cutting in.

Paint Kettles and Paint Trays

It is well worth investing in a paint kettle (a small plastic or aluminium can with a handle) if you are using a paint brush, as it is much more convenient than carrying a whole tin of paint around while you work. Before you begin work, put down thick layers of newspaper or a dust sheet, and open the tin in this area as a precautionary measure. Mix the paint thoroughly in the tin, then simply pour a little paint into the kettle, put the lid back on your paint tin, and hold the paint kettle by the handle as you work. This way, the paint dries out less quickly and there will be far less waste and mess if the kettle gets knocked over than if you spilt a whole tin of paint. For large areas, you will probably need to top up the kettle now and again.

Rollers need to be used with a tray that is a little wider than the sleeve. Roller trays have a reservoir for holding the paint and a raised, textured area, for distributing paint evenly over the roller.

Paint pads are also used with a tray, and some designs have a wheel at one end that helps to distribute paint evenly onto the pad.

Paint Pads

Ideal for flat surfaces, these can be used in a similar way to a roller. Available in a range of different sizes, the frame can be bought separately from the pads, and the pads are replaceable and relatively inexpensive. Small pads are ideal for more detailed work, and are a good option for cutting in, although a traditional paint brush will be easier to use if the area you are painting has uneven surfaces.

Wallpaper Stripping

There are now tools available that make stripping old wallpaper a straightforward job. Hand-held wallpaper strippers with a roller at the back help you to hold the blade at the correct angle. For stubborn paper there are electric steam strippers with a plate that you hold against the wall to melt the adhesive. If washable papers have been used in a kitchen or bathroom, a serrated scraper can be used to abrade the surface of the paper; this allows water to penetrate so that the paper is easier to remove.

✳ Basic Tools

- ✔ PAINT BRUSHES
- ✔ ROLLER
- ✔ PAINT PADS
- ✔ PAINT KETTLES AND TRAYS
- ✔ WALLPAPER STRIPPING TOOLS
- ✔ PAINT–STRIPPING TOOLS
- ✔ SANDING/SANDPAPER
- ✔ LADDERS, STEPS AND PLATFORMS
- ✔ DUST SHEETS

BRUSHES

It is useful to have a selection of brushes for different jobs

SCRAPERS

Multi-purpose knives (left), which can be used for stripping paper. A shave hook (right) is useful for stripping paint

ROLLERS

Use when painting larger areas

PAINT KETTLES

Transfer paint to a paint kettle, for ease of use while you work

HOT AIR GUN

Use this for softening and stripping paint

Sanding

The term 'sandpaper' is used to cover flexible backing sheets coated with abrasive grit on one side. This can be used to smooth many types of material, such as wood and plaster. Backing paper that is literally covered with grains of sand is no longer available commercially and backing sheets are now generally covered with grit made of glass, aluminium oxide, silicon carbide, or even garnet.

It is well worth having a few different grades of sandpaper on hand. As a general rule of thumb, the lower the number, the coarser and more abrasive they are. Use coarse grade paper for rough work such as scratching the surface of washable wallpaper and a fine grade for more delicate jobs such as sanding a newly-plastered area of the wall before painting it. Grades range from 40 (very coarse) to over 400 (very fine). Good quality sandpaper will have universally-sized grit. Each type of grit has different characteristics that make it suitable for specific applications. Individual sheets of sandpaper are normally marked on the reverse with the grit size or the grade.

Hot Air Scraper

Buy or rent a hot air scraper to soften old paint: this makes it easier to remove with a scraper (used for flat areas). You'll also need a shavehook, which is a three-pointed scraper used for detailed areas such as skirting boards and architrave.

SANDPAPER

The size of grit is used to classify the sandpaper by 'grade' as follows:

Grit size	Grade
40–60	very coarse
80–100	coarse
120–180	medium
240–320	fine
400+	very fine

IT'S A WRAP

If you anticipate doing a fair bit of sanding, invest in a sanding block (*right*). This is a piece of wood or cork that sandpaper can be wrapped around to make it easier to sand large areas. If you are sanding detailed areas such as mouldings, buy a flexible abrasive block, which can take the shape of the moulding.

Ladders, Steps and Platforms

A stepladder, or combination ladder, can be very useful when painting ceilings and, what's more, it will prove invaluable for areas such as hallways which have complex levels. If you have bought or hired a ladder it should be safely constructed, but always examine your ladder before every use and look closely at any moving parts. These can be damaged in transit or storage, so it's worth taking a minute or two to check them. Do not use a damaged ladder. Never paint a wooden ladder or trust a painted wooden ladder, as the paint may hide a structural flaw.

Before you begin work, always ensure that your ladders are fully extended and placed on a level surface, and invest in a ladder hook or shelf to hold your paint or tools. Make sure all locks are engaged and the ladder is supported securely at all contact points. Always check overhead clearance before using any ladder. You can construct a platform to work on by supporting a scaffolding plank between two step-ladders.

PLAN AHEAD
Always wear sensible footwear when working up a ladder and ensure the ladder is placed on an even surface (*above*).

CAUTION WORKING WITH LADDERS AND PLATFORMS

■ Wear non-slip shoes when working up a ladder, and do not stretch out too far or you could make it topple over.

■ Keep your body centred and move materials with extreme caution, always keeping one hand on the ladder.

■ Do not stand above the highest safe standing level of a ladder. These levels are: the second rung from the top of a stepladder, and the fourth rung from the top of an extension ladder.

Basic Tool Care and Overnight Storage

It is handy to have some cling film on hand to wrap around brushes, pads or rollers, in case you have to stop temporarily while you are working. This is fine overnight but is not recommended for more than 48 hours in total. For longer storage, clean your tools thoroughly.

Water-based paints can simply be washed off using water and mild detergent. Oil-based paints will need to be cleaned off using white spirit or thinner. You can buy brush combs from DIY stores, to separate any bristles that are stuck together with old paint.

doit CARE FOR YOUR BRUSHES

Brushes can be left temporarily during decorating but try to keep them free from dust and hairs.

Blot the wet brush on tissue paper to remove the excess moisture and avoid leaving brushes damp.

When you have completely finished painting, lay off the excess paint on an old cardboard box.

Remove any loose bristles by gently fanning the brush through your fingers as it is drying out.

You can simply run the brush under a cold tap for a few minutes to remove water soluble paints.

Invest in a purpose-built comb to ensure that the bristles on your paint brushes don't stick together.

Safety Equipment, Clothing and Dust Sheets

It's easy to get carried away with enthusiasm when you want to get cracking on a new project, but there are certain steps that it's wise to take before you begin.

When you buy or hire your tools, ask if there is safety equipment such as gloves, ear plugs or goggles that you need to use with them. Similarly, it is wise to wear gloves when dealing with caustic solutions such as paint stripper, so make sure you buy a suitable pair.

Finally, as well as protecting yourself, think about the surfaces you may need to cover up before you begin work. It is useful to invest in a dust sheet and a roll of masking tape, to fix it in place.

SAFE, NOT SORRY
It is not overly cautious to wear equipment such as goggles or a particle mask – they are a wise precaution and well worth using (*below*).

COVER UP
Thick dust sheets are available from DIY stores, or you might prefer to use an old sheet, folded over for extra thickness (*top*).

TAPE DOWN
When using dust sheets, ensure that they are right up against the wall you are painting, and use masking tape to secure the edges in place if necessary (*above*).

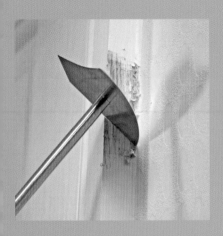
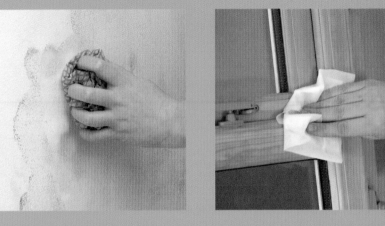

2 Preparation

Always take time to prepare surfaces thoroughly before starting work. It will be time well spent and will help you to achieve a professional finish.

Before You Begin

Removing Old Wallpaper

Depending on the type of wallpaper that has been used, it may be possible to remove it quite easily after soaking it with warm water to which you have added a squirt of washing-up liquid. Ensure the floor is adequately protected first, then you can simply spray the water on with a plant mister, or other hand-held spray.

Alternatively you can apply it to the walls with a damp sponge or cloth. Let the water soak in for around 30 minutes, then use a 4in (10cm) wide wallpaper stripper or scraper to peel the paper from the wall.

Always work from the bottom of the wall upwards and take care not to make nicks, or gouge holes in the plaster. Holding the stripper at an angle of about 30° to the wall surface is ideal. Occasionally apply more water if you notice that removal is getting harder.

Washable wallpaper, which is sometimes used in kitchens and bathrooms, can be more tricky to remove, as can wallpaper that has been painted over in the past. First you will need to score the surface with a serrated scraper, wire wool or coarse-grade sandpaper to allow water to penetrate and dissolve the adhesive.

WORK METHODICALLY
Wallpaper has a reputation for being difficult to put up and remove but, if you work methodically, it is surprisingly simple and you can achieve stunning results (*below*).

Try not to be too enthusiastic at this stage or you could go through and damage the wall – remember you are only grazing the surface of the paper to allow the water to soak through and do its job.

Vinyl or polyethylene wall coverings tend to be fairly easy to remove. Simply lifting a corner and pulling upwards may be all you need to do to remove a whole sheet. You will probably find that a backing paper has been left underneath. If it is in good condition, you may wish to re-use it as backing paper for your own decorating. If not, simply soak it and strip it away.

Extra Help

If, after giving the paper a good soak, you are still finding it really difficult to remove, you may well need to use a proprietary paint-stripping solution, or a steam stripper to soften the adhesive. A steam-stripping machine offers an effective way to remove stubborn wallpapers and is surprisingly easy to use. Although steam strippers are relatively inexpensive to purchase you might prefer to hire a machine. These tend to be more heavy duty than the less expensive models and can make the job much faster to complete.

When using a steam machine, always follow the manufacturer's instructions and do not add washing-up liquid to the water. The machine works by heating water and piping the resulting steam to a flat plate that you hold against the wall for a minute or so. The steam loosens the adhesive, allowing the paper to be removed with a scraper. Apply the steam plate to another area of wallpaper and repeat the process.

Wear a protective waterproof glove on the hand that is holding the stripper to avoid any burns or scalds.

It can be extremely satisfying to tear off big strips, but do take your time over this task and make a point of putting all the old paper in a bin liner as you go along. Be extra careful if you are working around details such as architrave and light fittings, to avoid damaging them.

✳ Golden Rules for Removing Wallpaper

✔ When removing wallpaper, work in good light and leave yourself plenty of time

✔ Don't get too carried away with the job in hand – if you damage the wall surface it can be time-consuming to repair

✔ Keep the wall wet, and allow around 30 minutes for the glue to dissolve

✔ Use a steam stripper if you find it hard going

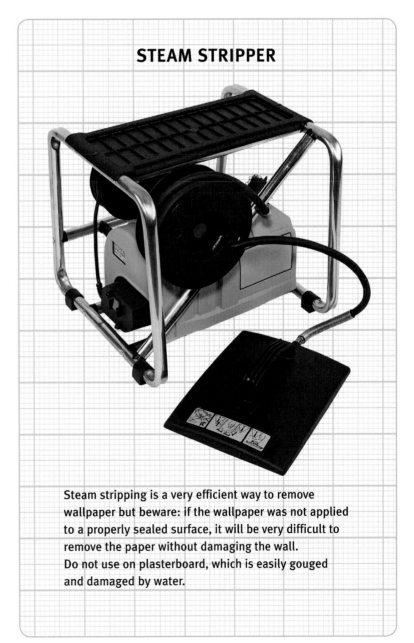

STEAM STRIPPER

Steam stripping is a very efficient way to remove wallpaper but beware: if the wallpaper was not applied to a properly sealed surface, it will be very difficult to remove the paper without damaging the wall.
Do not use on plasterboard, which is easily gouged and damaged by water.

Preparing the Walls for Painting

If the walls you intend to work on have already been painted and are in good condition, then minor filling and sanding is probably all that will be required before you start to paint. If a wall has been papered, after stripping it you will need to clean it with sugar soap. This is a powdered detergent that you mix with hot water and then apply with a sponge. After use, always rinse the wall well with clean water and allow it to dry thoroughly before you commence on the next stage of the work. If you wish to paint a previously wallpapered wall, use an oil-based undercoat first to prevent any traces of the adhesive bleeding through.

top tip*

Look out for caulks that can simply be over-painted when dry. Others may need an oil-based undercoat to prepare them for water-based paint so, if in doubt, ask at your local DIY store.

Simple Ways to Fill Holes and Cover Blemishes

Cracks

If you have a new house, or an older one that has recently been plastered, the chances are that there will be some cracks along the junctions of the ceilings and the walls. These are very simple to fill using flexible filler, which is known as caulk. You can buy it in a tube and you'll also need to get a separate dispenser (known as a sealant gun) that you can use to apply an even strip along the lines of the cracks. Use it sparingly and make sure that you smooth it with a damp sponge or a wetted fingertip before it dries, as it cannot be sanded away.

Minor Holes and Dents

If there are minor irregularities in the surface of your walls, it is a simple job to fill them. You can buy ready-mixed fillers in small amounts from all good DIY stores. First clean out the hole with a dusting brush, then press the filler into place using a filling knife. Most fillers tend to contract as they dry, so if you have a deep hole you may need to fill it twice. Aim to use enough filler for it to be slightly proud of the wall. Once it is completely dry, you can simply sand it with fine paper to create a smooth surface that is flush with the surrounding area.

REMOVING DUST

Sanding always produces dust, so get in the habit of always vacuuming it or brushing it away with a dusting brush as soon as you are finished. If the dust gets mixed in to your paint it will leave an uneven surface.

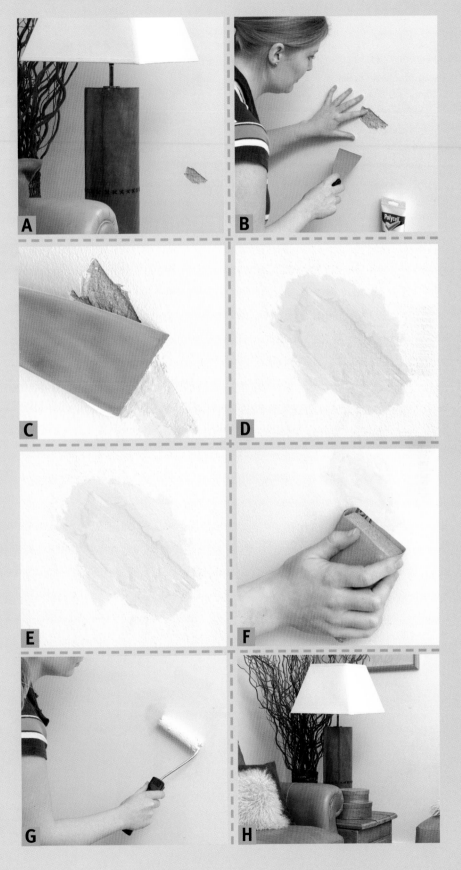 **do it** FILL MINOR HOLES

1 Small holes in the surface of your walls take minutes to remedy **A**.

2 Tubes of ready-made filler are widely available and easy to use **B**.

3 Use a putty knife to smooth a small amount of filler into the dent **C**.

4 Build up the filler until it is slightly proud of the wall's surface **D**.

5 As the filler dries it will change colour, so you know when to sand it **E**.

6 Use fine sandpaper to sand the filled area till it is flush with the wall **F**.

7 You can now paint straight over the filled area using a brush or roller **G**.

8 When the paint is dry, a well-made repair will be completely invisible **H**.

A

B

C

D

E

F

G

H

Larger Flaws

GET THE KNACK

There is a knack to applying plaster, but don't panic, if you only have a small area to do. Smooth it in different directions, with a float, until you get a satisfatory finish. Then, wet the blade, and go over the plaster again.

If you have larger cracks and holes, you may have to use plaster rather than filler and do a thorough patching job. Fortunately modern 'one-coat' plaster is quite simple to use and you can buy options that dry to a convenient white finish.

The first step is to remove all of the loose plaster, until you are back to the original sub-structure. Wet the area thoroughly with a damp sponge and paint on a PVA bonding agent. Mix the plaster with water into a thick, creamy paste and use a plasterer's trowel to apply it. If you need to do this in a series of layers, allow each one to dry out thoroughly in between, aiming to finish slightly proud of the existing plasterwork.

Then, when it is nearly dry, smooth and harden off with a plasterer's float that you have run under a tap to moisten the blade.

If you find there are a number of larger holes and cracks to fill, it might be worth calling in a professional plasterer, who can assess whether the plaster has 'blown', i.e. the base coat has become detached from the wall behind it, and could crumble away at any time. If you wish to check this yourself, gently knock the wall with your knuckles – you'll find that the blown areas have a more hollow resonance than sound plaster, in which case it may be necessary to skim the whole wall, or even re-plaster the room. This is not an easy job and it is one that is best left to the professionals.

doit OVERPAINT A DARK AREA

1 Applying a base coat will allow you to use light-coloured paint over a darker shade **A**.

2 There are options available that will give you dense coverage in just one coat **B**.

3 Apply using a roller with a smooth sleeve, as this helps you to get an even finish **C**.

4 Work the base coat evenly across the wall, rolling backwards and forwards **D**.

5 Once the base coat is fully dry, you can cover it with an emulsion top coat **E**.

6 Base coats also cover hairline cracks and minor dents, leaving a smooth surface **F**.

doit SEAL DAMP PATCHES

1 This wall suffers from a severe damp problem, which needs urgent attention **A**.

2 Wash the wall down with a recommend fungicide compound, to remove the bulk of the fungal spores **B**.

3 Apply damp-sealing paint in two coats, working thoroughly to ensure good coverage, then leave to dry **C**.

4 Once the wall is completely dry, you can apply emulsion by brush or roller, and the job is complete **D**.

toptip*

Damp on ceilings or the upper part of walls may indicate that your gutters are blocked or damaged, so get your roof checked, if necessary.

Undercoat

It is possible to paint directly over new plaster that is in good condition, if you use good quality paint. Alternatively, you may prefer to apply a 'mist coat' of emulsion, using one part water to ten parts paint. This mist coat is also known as primer. If a surface has been previously painted, you only need to patch-prime the sanded and filled areas.

Dry-lined walls and ceilings should be coated with special sealer before you apply emulsion, otherwise you may find that the paint will dry differently on the board and the jointing compound. Bear in mind that water-based paints tend to be applied in as many coats as necessary to provide an even coverage, so with these an undercoat is rarely used.

Masking and Protecting Carpets and Furniture

If it is practical, it's a good idea to remove all furniture and floor coverings from a room before you begin to decorate it. If not, ensure that you thoroughly cover anything you can't remove. Decorating can be a messy job and the odd paint spill or drip is almost inevitable. If you are painting a ceiling, tiny droplets of paint can fall all over the room. Plastic dust sheets can be used over furniture and fabric dust sheets can be used on wooden or washable floors and these will protect against minor spills.

If you have carpet on the floor, take extra care to ensure that an impermeable dust sheet is held firmly behind the carpet edge with masking tape. This tape is also ideal for using on the edges of woodwork such as skirting boards and architraves. It peels off easily, taking any small spills or smudges with it.

If you are planning to wallpaper a room, ensure you have finished all the paintwork first, as even gentle masking tape can stain or tear the paper.

PROTECT THE FLOOR
Even if you are only painting a small area of the room, it is well worth taking time to protect the floor with dust sheets (*right*).

Treating Wooden Surfaces

Painted or varnished doors, windows, mouldings, beams and furniture can all be stripped back to the bare wood, either to create a natural look, or to reveal the original detail again if it has been obscured under multiple layers of paint.

In the 1960s older properties were sometimes 'modernized' by covering old beams with plasterboard. If you suspect the beams in your home have been covered in this way, cut a neat, easily-repaired hole in the plasterbboard to have a look.

SIMPLY NATURAL
Beams, floors and furniture can all look wonderful when stripped and either left looking natural or enhanced with wax, oil or varnish (*left*).

A SPECIAL AFFINITY
Leather sofas and chairs look particularly good on a sanded wooden floor (*left and below*).

✳ Tools for Wood

✔ Wood stripper of choice

✔ Methylated spirits
(if using solvent stripper)

✔ Dust sheets

✔ Paint kettle

✔ Old paint brush

✔ Scraper

✔ Grade 4 or 5 wire wool

✔ White vinegar
(if using caustic stripper)

✔ Shavehook
(for fiddly parts)

CAUTION USING CHEMICAL STRIPPER

■ CHEMICAL STRIPPING is generally considered to offer the best possible result, it is quicker at removing finishes than sanding alone, and tends to be more gentle on the wood. However, chemical strippers are hazardous, so care must be taken at all times: eye protection is absolutely essential, so wear appropriate safety goggles, and chemical-resistant gloves that will not dissolve.

■ SOLVENT STRIPPERS are very gentle and won't discolour the wood, so they are recommended for stripping delicate wood such as antique furniture. They may work out more expensive to use than caustic strippers.

As solvent strippers are relatively mild, you will probably need to use more than one application, and this means you might get through a fair bit of stripper.

■ CAUSTIC STRIPPERS will remove most finishes and are good on thick paint build-up, but they are less gentle on the wood than solvent strippers and, unless they are used very carefully, they can lead to cracks appearing on older wood.

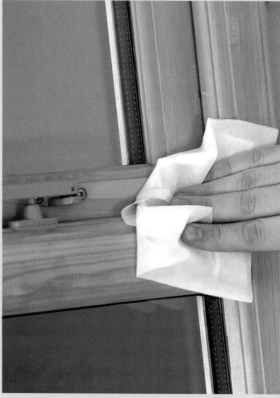

BACK TO BASICS
Stripper makes good use of an old brush (*far left*). After using a solvent stripper, return the wood to a neutral pH balance by wiping it over with a little methylated spirit (*left*).

 **STRIP WOOD**

1 Painted doors often hide beautiful pine underneath, especially in older homes. Before starting work, cover all surrounding areas with thick dust sheets, and always keep a cloth handy to remove any spills **A**.

2 Wearing chemical-resistant gloves, pour a little stripper into a chemical-resistant kettle, then use an old paint brush or coarse wire wool to paint a layer over the surface of the wood. Always read the label and follow the safety instructions on the product you choose. It may be necessary to use a respirator **B**.

3 If using a solvent stripper, it will start to work in a few minutes and you will see the surface of the paint bubbling. If using a caustic stripper, you may need to leave it overnight, covered with polythene to stop it drying out **C**.

4 Use a scraper to gently remove the soft layer of paint, and a shave-hook to gently scrape away softened paint from the more fiddly parts of the wood. If using a solvent stripper, it will probably be necessary to apply at least one more coat of stripper, and let it soak in for five minutes **D**.

5 Once you can see the bare wood underneath, remove the remaining paint with number 4 or number 5 grade wire wool. Use firm strokes, in the direction of the grain. Once the wood is bare and not waxy, neutralize solvent stripper by rubbing the wood with a cloth dipped in white spirit or methylated spirit. If you used caustic stripper, then give it a thorough scrub with white vinegar to neutralize it **E**.

6 The finished door is now ready for sanding. You may prefer to finish it with oil, wax or varnish, depending on the style of your home **F**.

A

B

C

D

E

F

Sanding Wooden Surfaces

A PRACTICAL SOLUTION
Wooden floors have
an unrivalled natural
beauty, and they
are relatively easy
to maintain.

If you are lucky enough to have original
wooden floors in your home, chances are
you will want to strip some of them to show
off their natural beauty. Machine sanding
is a good option if your floor is in relatively
good condition, but be warned: sanding
can be a messy job, and it is hard work,
so make it easier for yourself by hiring
the best possible sander and edger
you can afford, with a dust extractor.
Changing the sandpapers is a time-
consuming and expensive business, and
using cheaper papers is a false economy,
so invest in very good quality (zirconia)
abrasive paper.

✱ Tools for Sanding

✔ Sander and edger of choice, with dust extractor

✔ Pliers

✔ Zirconia abrasive paper

✔ Ear plugs (sanders make a lot of noise)

✔ Dust mask

✔ Hammer

✔ Nail punch

toptip*

Ask the hire shop if you can return papers that you don't use and, if so, buy more than you think you'll need. That way, if you run out, you won't have to stop work to go to the shop and buy some more.

SIZE MATTERS
Belt sander for large areas (*below left*), and edge sander for more tricky areas (*below right*).

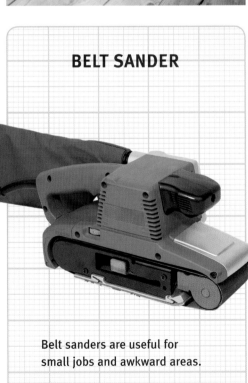

BELT SANDER

Belt sanders are useful for small jobs and awkward areas.

doit SAND A FLOOR

1 Working methodically from one side of the room to the other, remove as many nails, tacks and screws as possible, then use a punch to push any you can't remove to a depth of at least 1/8 in (3mm) below the surface. This will help to avoid damaging the abrasive sheet **A**.

2 When you have checked over the whole floor, start from a different side of the room and go over it all again, until you are certain you have dealt with each nail.

3 Now tape polythene dustsheets across stairwells and doorways and use masking tape around door edges. Time spent doing this will save you time vacuuming sawdust from other rooms in the house for weeks to come. Open the windows as wide as you can.

4 For the preliminary sand, use a large belt sander. Start with 24 grit paper for heavily soiled or uneven pine floors, 40 grit for normal pine floors and 40 or 50 grit for soft pine or parquet. Work through the grades not missing out more than one grade in between, finishing off with 100 or 120 grit. Sweep and vacuum in between grades to avoid contamination with the coarser grits. Do the same with the edger which gives you a finer result **B**.

5 Sand in the direction of the boards at a very slight angle to the horizontal and then reverse the direction of cut with alternate grades. This will help you to ensure you are removing the marks left by the sander.

6 Remove all the old finish and discolouration with the coarsest grade, as you will not be able to clean the floor with the lighter grades.

7 Finish off perfectly straight with the finer grades of paper.

8 Scrape out the corners and around radiators with a cabinet scraper and finish off with a detail sander – a useful machine for small or difficult areas **C**.

9 Before staining, waxing or varnishing, run over the floor with a damp rag dipped in methylated spirits. This is the best way to remove the last vestiges of dust for a fine finish.

toptip*

You can keep dust levels in the room down by emptying the dust bags regularly when less than a third full. Before undoing the bag from the machine, cover the whole dust bag with a bin bag. and then undo the dust bag inside it, keeping it closed as tightly as you can.

A

B

C

WORK IN PROGRESS

First use a belt sander with large bag to capture dust (*above left*), then a rotary sander, to achieve a fine finish (*above right*).

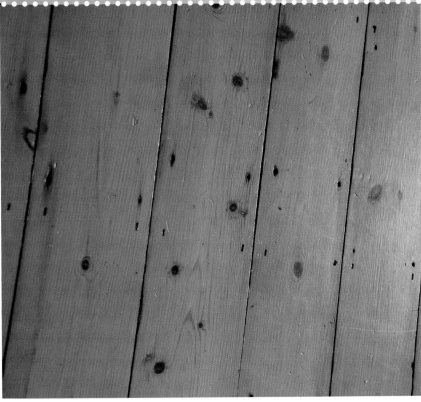

THE FINAL RESULT

A beautifully sanded and waxed floor makes all your labours worthwhile (*left*).

Finishing

CHOOSE CAREFULLY
Waxed floors look fantastic, but they do need regular maintenance, so you may prefer to reserve this look for bedrooms and use varnish on floors in busy areas such as the hallway.

Waxing

Wax is available in several colours, and can give a warm, mellow look to newly sanded floors or other woodwork. Wax is a better option than varnish if you want a natural look, but waxed floors will require more maintenance, so you may prefer to use varnish on floors in heavy-traffic areas. You can buy water- or solvent-based seals to prepare your wood before waxing.

Follow the manufacturer's instructions with regards to drying times before you apply any finish as these can vary. If your wood has been sealed with water-based seal, only finish it with water-based wax as solvents can damage the seal. Regularly polish waxed floors and reapply a layer of wax as necessary. To prevent build-up of wax, you can wash them with a neutral detergent.

Oiling

Oils have traditionally been used to protect timber for many years and you will have a number of options to choose from if you select this finish. Be warned, however, that oils darken the wood and this finish is inclined to trap dust, so it is not ideal in areas with an open fire, for example, or for floors in heavy traffic areas. You will need to clean oiled surfaces regularly. If your oiled floor looks dull, rub it over with a scouring pad and then reapply the oil with a soft cloth.

Varnishing

Varnishes are the most popular choice of treatment for wooden surfaces, especially since the advent of water-based seals. They are a better option than solvent-based varnishes as the latter not only smell unpleasant, they can take a long time to dry so, if you need to apply two or three coats, the room is out of bounds for a long time. In contrast, water-based varnishes can be dry within three hours. You can choose from matt, satin and gloss finishes and all of them will alter the colour of the timber slightly, as they change the way it absorbs light.

Staining

Stains can be applied to most timbers – look out for a water-based stain if you require an even and natural finish. Bear in mind that there is no turning back once you have applied a stain to your wood, so test a little on an offcut of timber, or an inconspicuous area, before using it on a floor or valuable piece of furniture. Check the packaging to ensure that the stain you choose is compatible with any finishing or sealing product that you have used. It's also worth knowing that stains often look dark when applied, and then dry to a lighter finish.

ALTERNATIVE CHOICE
Water-based varnishes dry quickly and come in a variety of different finishes.

Dado Rails

Back in the 1700s it was considered fashionable to arrange furniture around the outside edge of the room. Chairs would be lined up with their backs against the wall, and tables and other furnishings would also be abutted up against it.

Dado rails were originally invented simply to protect the wall, which could easily have been chipped, scratched or gouged as people sat down on the chairs, or moved furniture around. These rails were typically employed at the level of the top of the chair back, and proved to be a very practical measure. However, as their popularity increased, it didn't take long before people started to recognize their potential as a decorative feature.

Today, dado rails still serve their original practical function, especially in dining rooms and living rooms, where it is usual to have furniture sited up against a wall.

If you are choosing a table and set of chairs, it is well worth taking the height of your dado rails into account. Alternatively, it may be possible to move the rail to suit the height of your chair backs.

EVEN MORE PRACTICAL
Here the wainscot panelling serves a similar purpose to a dado rail but, extending to the floor, is even more practical, as well making an attractive feature *(left)*.
Dado rails provide a great opportunity to use different colours and wallcoverings in a room *(facing page, top and right)*.

DADO RAIL VARIATIONS
Four different styles of commonly available dado rail

Changing Times

When Queen Victoria was crowned, the fashion changed and furniture was more likely to be grouped in the centre of the room, much as it is now. However, people were still keen to have dado rails and so even up to around 1870, most new homes that were built would have featured these designs. As the century came to a close, fashions changed again and people wanted more simple, streamlined looks in their homes, and rails became less commonly used.

By the late 1900s new homes would generally only have been built with a dado rail in high-traffic areas such as the hall, stairs and landings and these were vulnerable to being knocked by people carrying water and coal around the house. The dado rail persisted in the hall, staircase and landing through the Edwardian period, then well into the 1920s.

Nowadays, it is quite common for modern homes to feature a dado rail in halls, living rooms and dining rooms, although they tend to be less popular in bedrooms.

In some period homes the dado rails may have been removed during the 1960s and '70s, when there was a trend for these properties to be 'modernized.' However, many people are now choosing to put them back.

MIX MOULDINGS
Dado rails can be combined with other decorative elements on your walls such as architrave and panelling.

DECORATIVE AND FUNCTIONAL

Now used as a decorative feature, dado rails were first used to protect walls from being scraped by chair backs (*below*).

toptip*

As well as protecting the wall from knocks and scrapes, dado rails bring a decorative element to a room, allowing you to paint it in different colours below and above the rail. This also serves a practical purpose, as it is often the lower part of a wall that gets scuffed by children or pets and when you are moving furniture. If you have a dado rail in place, you can simply repaint the lower area, if the upper section is still pristine.

As well as being practical, picture rails emphasize the feeling of height in a room and can be highlighted in a contrasting colour for a sophisticated look. Here they are not used for their original purpose, but serve as a dramatic feature (*below*).

Picture Rails

If you are fortunate enough to have tall ceilings in your home, you may also have picture rails. These mouldings became popular during the mid-nineteenth century, when they were used to separate off the upper wall, or frieze.

As the name suggests, the rails were used to hang pictures, and special hooks were designed that could simply be looped over the rail. Wire or chain would be used to affix the pictures to the hooks, which had the great advantage that pictures could easily be hung and moved without damaging the wall behind. In the 1920s and '30s this rail was often replaced by a narrow shelf, which was generally used to support plates and other decorative items – you often see similar shelves in kitchens today.

Many older homes retain their original picture rails but they can also be very effective when added to give a wall the illusion of height, or to add interest to the design of the room.

Skirting Boards

Of all the different decorative mouldings, the skirting board does, perhaps, serve the most practical functions: it covers the gap where the plaster of the wall meets the floor, so helping to keep out draughts and protecting the plaster from knocks, and it also sets off the decorative role of the wallpaper or paint. Most homes built today feature skirting of some sort.

In the past, these mouldings were used as a statement about the status of the home and its owners. The more grand the house, and the room in it, the more elaborate and therefore costly the moulding would be. Reception rooms and areas where guests would see the mouldings tended to feature complex designs that were often up to 18in (45cm) tall. Bedrooms would have had rather more understated designs. In homes built today, skirting may be only 4in (10cm) tall, but it still serves a very useful purpose.

OGEE AND TORUS SKIRTING

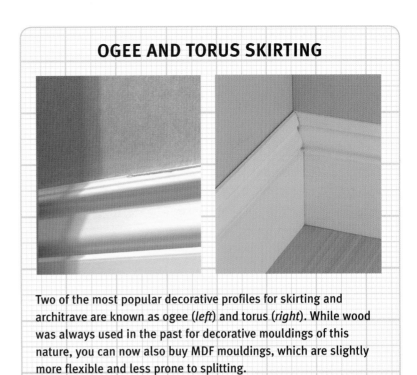

Two of the most popular decorative profiles for skirting and architrave are known as ogee (*left*) and torus (*right*). While wood was always used in the past for decorative mouldings of this nature, you can now also buy MDF mouldings, which are slightly more flexible and less prone to splitting.

A FINISHING TOUCH
Skirting boards hide the space between the floor and the wall, making a room look finished as well as helping to keep out drafts (*left*).

Architraves

The architrave is the moulding around a door or window. As with other mouldings, an older home is likely to feature larger and more elaborate designs, especially in the more public rooms. The architrave covers the joint between the door or window-lining and the wall, and usually has less depth than matching skirting boards.

CHOICE OF MATERIAL
Used around doors and windows, architraves were traditionally made of wood, but are now available in a range of materials, including MDF (*below*).

ARCHITRAVE VARIATIONS

Visit a number of timber and DIY stores if you want to see the largest available choice

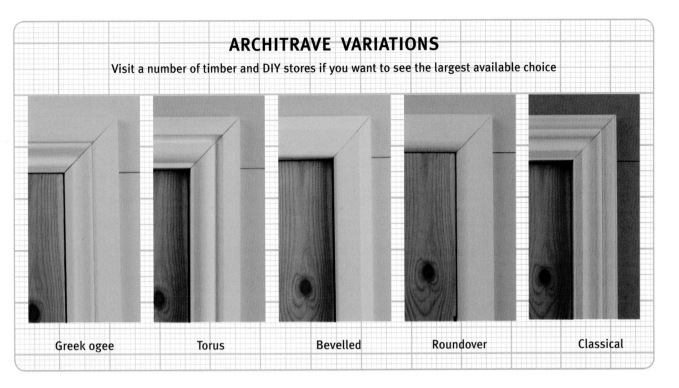

| Greek ogee | Torus | Bevelled | Roundover | Classical |

STYLISH ADDITION
Architraves add a certain
grandeur to any doorway
(*left and above*).

Care of Mouldings

MAKE A FEATURE
You can strip mouldings such as skirting back to bare wood, or emphasize them with a coat of paint (*below*).

If you have the original wooden mouldings in your home, you may choose to strip them back to bare wood and then stain, varnish, or wax them.

Alternatively, you might prefer to paint the mouldings with white – or even coloured – gloss paint, which is very easy to wipe down with a damp sponge, if they become dusty or scuffed.

If you are planning to repaint your mouldings, it is probably not necessary to strip them back to bare wood, unless there are so many layers of paint on them that the details are obscured. You may simply need to sand the mouldings with a flexible block and use a vacuum and damp sponge to remove any dust and debris before you begin to paint.

Ceiling Roses

In the past, more affluent properties would traditionally have featured a ceiling rose in the centre of the main reception rooms, but they are less commonly used in modern houses. If you have the originals in your home, they may need to have the paint carefully stripped away before you can repaint them. If you want to add a centrepiece to your room, try to match it as closely as possible to your existing mouldings. If you are unsure about which style would be appropriate, it may be worth looking in a similar house in your area to see if they have original mouldings that you can emulate.

A STYLISH TOUCH
Even a simple ceiling rose looks impressive when a candelabra is hung from it (*left*).

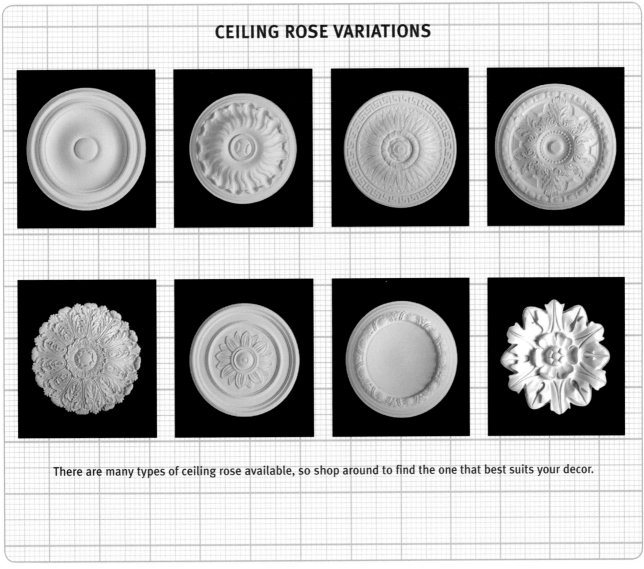

CEILING ROSE VARIATIONS

There are many types of ceiling rose available, so shop around to find the one that best suits your decor.

Buying Mouldings

ADD VARIETY
Mouldings come in many shapes and sizes. Aim to choose a style suited to the age of your home – so, for a 1920's property, choose an Art Deco finish (*below*).

If you are buying more mouldings to match existing ones in your home, try to take a piece of the original with you to your DIY store so that you can match the profile. Two of the most popular decorative profiles for skirting and architrave are ogee and torus. If the shop does not have the profile you require, it may be possible to find it in a reclaim yard or from a specialist.

While wood was always used in the past for decorative mouldings, such as skirting boards, you can now also buy MDF mouldings that are slightly more flexible and less prone to splitting.

Ceiling roses are available in polystyrene, fibreglass, plaster, glass-reinforced plastic or resin. It's worth investing in the better quality models if you want a more authentic look.

Fitting Mouldings

Fixing wooden mouldings requires accurate measurement and very precise joints. Fixing it securely and neatly can be tricky, so get someone to help you hold the moulding steady while you draw marker lines with soft pencil on the walls.

CAUTION USE A DETECTOR

■ Before nailing or screwing any mouldings into the wall, use a detector to check that there are no hidden pipes or cables behind the areas where you are working. These are not expensive to buy from DIY shops, but can also be hired.

MEASURE CAREFULLY
Preparing mouldings for areas such as the inside of a bay window requires careful measurement and accurate cuts (*left*).

doit FIT A CEILING ROSE

1 To fit a centrepiece, first hold it in position and mark right round it. Use a detector to locate the ceiling joists.

2 Mark the position on the ceiling using a soft pencil, so that it is easy to remove any marks left if you change your mind.

3 If a light fitting is intended to run through the centre of the rose, drill a hole to the appropriate width, ready to thread the wire through when fitting the rose.

4 If there are no ready-made screw holes in the centrepiece, make them in an unobtrusive area.

5 Use the recommended coving adhesive on the back of the rose, and align the drill holes with the joists before you push it firmly against the ceiling.

6 Ask someone to hold it in place for you while you use wood screws to screw it to the ceiling joists. Wait until the adhesive is dry before you fix the light fitting in place.

Coving

This is the concave curved surface between the wall and ceiling of a room. To fit coving, first check its depth on the packaging. Use this measurement to draw a horizontal guide line on the wall with a soft pencil where the lower edge of the coving will sit. You can use the same measurement and an offcut of coving to mark a mirroring line along the ceiling. When you have the position fully marked out, apply adhesive to the back of the coving, along the upper and lower edges.

Next, press it into place, using your pencil marks as a guide. If excess adhesive spills out over the edges, simply wipe it away with a lightly dampened sponge. The adhesive takes a while to dry properly, so it is sensible to use fixings to hold the coving in place, especially at the joins where the two lengths meet. When you reach a corner the edge will need to be 'mitred' – cut at the appropriate angle to meet the other corner piece (see facing page).

SIMPLE FIXING
Details such as coving can be simply secured in place with adhesive. There are many options available (*below*).

do it MITRE JOINTS

1 When fitting mouldings to the corner of a wall you will need to make an angled cut. Mitring gives neat joints in a corner, or between lengths along a straight run on a wall.

2 You will need to mitre a different angle for internal and external corners. You can use a mitre block to cut skirting, rails and architrave.

3 Simply place the moulding in the block with its back edges flush to the block, then slide your saw into the guide slots to ensure you cut the ends at the right angle.

4 If you have a lot of cuts to do, you may prefer to buy or rent a mitre saw, which can cut at a precise angle.

MEASURE CAREFULLY
To achieve a really professional finish like this when fitting skirting, great care with measurements is required (*left*).

Skirting Boards

The method you choose to apply these mouldings depends on your type of wall.

Stud Wall

If you are fixing skirting to a simple timber stud wall, first locate the position of each stud using a detector. Then you can apply grab adhesive to the back of the board, place it in position and then fix it in place with two screws or lost-head nails at each stud.

Lath and Plaster

For older property, with lath and plaster walls, first locate the vertical studs using a detector, then mark their positions on the wall using a soft pencil. Apply grab adhesive to the back of the board and use lost-head nails or screws to fix it in position. If you cannot locate the studs, simply fix the skirting at regular intervals.

Brick Walls

Fixing boards to a masonry wall is slightly more complex. First apply grab adhesive to the back of the board and place it in position. Use a masonry drill to make pilot holes at intervals of around 1ft (30cm). Next, enlarge the openings of the holes with a countersink bit. This will allow the screw heads to sit below the surface of the wood. Insert a masonry wall plug into each hole. These help to support the screw in the masonry. Finally screw the boards to the wall. You can fill the holes with coloured filler and then sand them if you prefer.

Once you have fixed the first corner piece in place, check that the second piece fits before applying wood glue to the cut end. Position the other piece and then wipe away excess glue with a damp sponge. For a secure finish, drill pilot holes for two panel pins to fit through the mitred joint and hold it together, then pin the corner.

COUNTERSINK
Countersink the holes in the skirting, so that the plugs and screwheads are sunk in a little and you can apply filler afterwards (*right*).

CHECK FIRST
Always use a metal detector to check for hidden pipes or cables before starting work (*right*). Apply a regular pattern of adhesive to the back of the skirting board, so that it adheres properly to the wall (*below*).

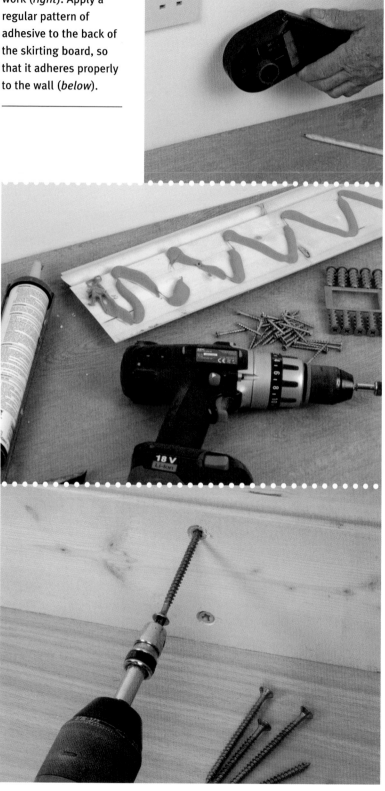

After you have screwed skirting boards into place, use a little filler to conceal the holes, sand the area and then paint the boards for a stylish finish.

3 Paints and Painting

Paint is inexpensive, easy to apply and can transform a room in just a day or two once you know how to apply it. Choose it carefully, to create the effect you want.

Choosing Different Paints

Paints are made up of pigments that are applied to surfaces with a binding agent. They tend to be known as either water-based or oil-based (emulsion or gloss) depending on the binding agent used. The latter often use white spirit or thinner as a binder and so you need to use the same solvent with them for washing the brushes.

The type of paint you choose depends on the surface you are covering and the finish you require. There are specialist options available for walls, floors, woodwork and other surfaces such as tiles. Environmentally friendly paints are now available, and these are also kinder to your health.

A SOOTHING EFFECT
The cool blue emulsion used on these walls gives the room a very restful feel (*left*).

Water-based Paints or 'Emulsions'

A QUIRKY TOUCH
Here the pale green-painted boarding and dark blue refrigerator make for a delightfully quirky room (*below*).

As the name implies, these are made using water, and are often referred to as emulsions. Emulsions tend to dry quickly, they don't smell unpleasant and they usually have less impact on the environment than solvent-based paints.

A popular choice for interior walls and ceilings, you can now also find water-based paints that can be used on wood and metal surfaces. Many types of finish are available, including dead-flat matt, matt,

silk and satin. Alternatively, there is water-based eggshell paint, if you prefer. It is also worth bearing in mind that emulsions are 'breathable' – which means that both air and moisture can pass through them – and this helps to avoid problems with blistering and peeling. These paints are recommended for use in older homes. During the clean-up stage of painting, brushes and rollers can be easily cleaned with soap and water.

FRESH AND AIRY
Emulsions dry
quickly and do not
generally have an
unpleasant smell,
especially important
in a bedroom (*right*).

**To help ensure an even
finish when touching
up, be sure to use the
same tool that you
used when you first
applied the paint.**

CHOOSE THE RIGHT PAINT
Gloss paints offer a tough, waterproof finish (*above left*). Primers can give you better adhesion to impervious surfaces such as the UPVC on window frames (*left*). Primers are useful on bare surfaces such as wood, or metal (*above*).

Oil or Solvent-based Paints, or 'Gloss'

Gloss paints are often oil- or solvent-based, and these binding agents have very good adhesive properties. They provide a very tough, durable finish to both wood and metal and are usually dirt and water resistant. However, glossed surfaces can become brittle and crack over time, the paints are slower to dry than emulsions, and they tend to have a noticeable chemical smell.

Brushes used with solvent-based paints need to be cleaned with white spirit or turpentine after use. They may only last for a short while, even with proper care.

Primers

These should be used on interior and exterior bare surfaces such as wood, walls and metal. They are also useful for giving better adhesion to impervious surfaces such as tiles, melamine and plastics.

Primers tend to be labelled 'interior only', 'exterior only', or 'universal' which is the best option if you want to paint surfaces in both areas, such as both sides of your front door. Primers help the top coat to stick to the surface and can also help to prevent stains from bleeding through. If you are priming metal, look for anti-corrosion and anti-rust properties on the can. For walls look out for a 'primer sealer'.

If you're unsure whether a primer is needed on an already painted surface, press a piece of transparent tape onto the old paint, then remove it – if the paint comes off it needs priming.

Undercoats

These can be useful on interior and exterior wood and metal, as they both cover up stains and provide an even base for topcoats. It can be useful to use a slightly different shade of undercoat to topcoat, so you can see where a surface has been painted. When painting wood, ensure you use a water-based undercoat, as this will be flexible and resist cracking and flaking.

Textured Paints

This option contains elements such as sand or tiny beads that provide thicker paint, which has a rough texture on application. Textured paints offer an interesting finish and can be helpful for covering cracks and minor imperfections. They are best applied with a roller to walls and ceilings.

PREPARE CAREFULLY
Water-based undercoats are ideal for wood, as they provide a flexible base for the topcoat (*right*). Textured paints are useful for uneven surfaces (*below*).

One-coat Paints

As the name suggests, these are thick, high quality options that are designed to need only a single coat, making the process of painting walls and ceilings faster. However, bear in mind that even with these paints, one coat is unlikely to be enough if you are covering a dark colour with a much lighter paint. Gloss versions are also available for wood.

THE QUICKEST COURSE
If you are decorating in a hurry, look out for one-coat paints (*below*).

Paints for Specific Areas

Ceiling Paints

Special ceiling paints are available which are thicker than standard emulsion, so they are less likely to spatter and drip. They are often solid and come in a tray, ready to be applied with a roller.

Floor Paints

Different ranges are available for use on wooden floorboards and concrete. These durable finishes are designed to withstand heavy wear and tear. Best applied with a roller, they can be water- or solvent-based coverings, and they usually have a low-sheen finish.

A FRESH TOUCH
Painted white floorboards are fresh and practical (*below*).

AVOID DRIPS
If you are worried about drips and spatters, look out for ceiling paints which are extra thick and designed to go on smoothly (*below*). Applying floor paints with a roller is a surprisingly quick job (*bottom*).

Kitchen and Bathroom Paints

Walls and ceilings in kitchens, bathrooms and utility rooms – or any area that becomes steamy or damp – can be prone to being stained with dark mould. There are specialist paints available which contain fungicide to deter mould growth, and many can be wiped clean. Prepare areas and remove any surface mould before using these paints, by wiping over with a diluted bleach solution, then rinse and allow to dry thoroughly before painting.

EASY CLEAN

Rooms that are subjected to lots of steam, such as kitchens and bathrooms, can benefit from a specialist paint that offers a wipe-clean surface (*right, below*).

Nursery Paints

You can now buy low-odour, quick-drying paints that are formulated to be durable enough to use in children's rooms. Often acrylic-based, these paints allow surfaces to be wiped clean and they can also withstand a few minor knocks and bumps. Bear in mind that they need to dry thoroughly for at least a fortnight before you wipe them for the first time.

BE PRACTICAL
In children's rooms you might want to use low-odour paints that will forgive a little inevitable wear and tear (*below*).

Types of Traditional Paint

MILK PAINTS give a matt finish.
LIMEWASH offers an aged effect.
DISTEMPER creates a powdery finish and is often used on furniture to create an aged effect or on ceilings or plaster mouldings.

Traditional Paints

Mainly water based, there are various types of historic paints which are suitable for use on period homes as they allow the walls to 'breathe' i.e. let air and moisture pass through the surface.

RUSTIC EFFECT
These shabby-chic, limewashed walls are right up to date, and create a pleasing rustic feel (*right*).

'Green' Paints

Ordinary paints are manufactured from complex, synthetic chemicals. Many of these can be damaging to your health or the environment.

Environmentally friendly or 'green' paints are made of renewable materials such as plant oils. They contain fewer preservatives and artificial chemicals and can be made via a process that has less impact on the environment. They are ideal for use in children's rooms and are a sensible choice for anyone who has breathing difficulties or asthma.

GO GREEN

'Green' paints are kinder to you and the environment. Available in a huge selection of colours and finishes, they are becoming increasingly popular.

Why Use 'Green' Paints?

Headaches and allergies are common side-effects of decorating with ordinary paint, aside from more serious risks for the professional decorator. With no toxic by-products and no complex chemical processing, natural paints make very little impact on the environment. The fact that they are odour-free means that you can use them for decorating in winter, when you don't want to open windows and doors. What's more, they often cost the same as ordinary paints.

A COUNTRY STYLE
Environmentally
friendly paint is
especially suitable for
a family kitchen (*left*).

Specific-use Paints

Heat-resistant Paint

If you are painting radiators or pipes, choose a covering that has been specially designed so that it doesn't degrade or yellow at high temperatures. First ensure the area to be covered is cold, then apply the paint in thin layers. Ensure you do not cover areas such as control valves, which need to move freely.

RADIATORS

You can paint your radiators in a variety of colours, but ensure the surface is cold before you start work (*below left*). Cover areas such as valves with masking tape to ensure that they will be able to move freely after you have finished painting a radiator (*below*).

Surfaces that
are exposed to
the elements can
benefit from a regular
application of paint, to
keep them looking at
their best (*below*).

Masonry Paint

If you are painting exterior masonry,
render, pebbledash, concrete, or brick walls,
then you can choose specific paints in
either smooth or textured finishes. One-
coat products are also available. Some
contain fungicide to help prevent mould
growth, so look out for these if mould has
been a problem in the area you are working
on in the past.

top tip*

To check that the existing exterior paint is
stable, simply rub an area of the wall with a
dark-coloured cloth. If it picks up a chalky
deposit, it's best to scrub the wall with a
stiff brush, to remove any loose material
before painting.

Metal Paint

Designed to give protection to metal objects
such as gates, drainpipes and garage doors,
you can buy specialist metal paints in both
gloss and satin finishes. Before you begin
painting, it's worth spending a few minutes
using a wire brush to remove any rust. If
there are any pits or dents, you can fill them
with an epoxy-based filler that inhibits rust.
Use soapy water to remove any grease from
the surface of the metal and allow it to dry
thoroughly before painting. Spray paints are
available which may be more convenient for
small areas, but only use them in a well-
ventilated space. If spraying, wear protective
clothing (see page 53) and ensure that you
have masked off the surrounding areas.

APPLYING METAL PAINT
If you are spraying *in situ*, tape protective
covering to the surrounding area (*below*).

Painting Made Easy

Loading a Brush

When using a brush, dip it in to around a third of the bristle-length for water-based paint, or a quarter of the bristle length for oil-based paint, to avoid 'overloading'. Overloading a brush, roller or pad can lead to paint splattering, or running which will create more work for you in the long run. Scrape off the excess on each side of the brush across the rim of your paint kettle, then apply the paint to your surface, using random strokes in different directions. (See also 'Lay Off Paint' on page 106).

TECHNIQUE PAYS OFF
Stick to the simple guidelines *below*, and you can achieve superb results (*right*).

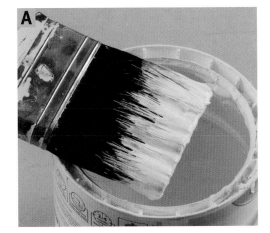

DO NOT OVERLOAD
Dip the brush in just so far **A**. Beware the overloaded brush **B**.

✳ To Achieve a Professional Finish

✔ Before you begin, thoroughly prepare the surfaces that are to be painted.

✔ Make sure you use the right type of paint for the surface and finish you require.

✔ Always paint in good light. Natural daylight is preferable and, if possible, avoid starting in daylight and finishing the job using artificial light.

✔ Try to finish each section, such as a wall or ceiling, in one session to avoid a dried line appearing.

✔ If you are using emulsion, it may be necessary to shut the windows before you begin work to prevent it from drying out too quickly.

✔ Take care to apply paint when it is not too hot or too cold to get the best results.

✔ Complete the coats on one surface before you move on to the next.

✔ Bear in mind that a wall might need a primer or undercoat before you apply a coat or two of emulsion.

✔ Always cut in first before you paint a large surface (see page 106).

✔ Before you begin work, open the lid of your paint tin with a screwdriver or blunt knife. Most paint will need to be stirred thoroughly to mix up all the ingredients. Failure to do this can lead to streaky surfaces and poor coverage.

✔ Keep doors and windows closed while working, if possible. Otherwise insects may fly onto your freshly painted surfaces.

Cutting In

This is the term applied to painting a strip that is roughly 2in (5cm) wide all around the perimeter of any large surfaces to be covered. For example, if you are painting a living room, you would cut in around the door frame, the windows, the ceiling, the light switches and any other features. It is relatively time-consuming and can take roughly as long as it does to fill in the larger areas, but it is well worth taking your time over this step, as cutting in hides any uneven edges caused by using a large paint brush, pad or roller. Cutting in should always be the first step before you paint any large surface.

Use a small brush around 1in (2.5cm) wide for this job. You may prefer to use one which has bristles cut at an angle.

TAKE THE TROUBLE
Cutting in takes time, but is well worth the trouble (*above*).
Stir your paint very thoroughly before you decant it, as the heavier ingredients can sink to the bottom of the tin (*right*).

doit 'LAY OFF' PAINT

To achieve a professional finish, it is a good idea to 'lay off' paint as you go along. When you have covered a small area, and most of the paint has come off your brush, simply glide it very gently over the area you have just painted, using the very tips of the bristles. This same technique can be used for pads or rollers too.

BEWARE OF TOO MUCH PAINT
Try not to have too much paint on your brush or you'll end up having to deal with runs and drips (*right*).

Get into the habit of painting each room in a particular order. For example, if you are repainting a room, it is best to start from the top and work down. Cover the ceiling first and then the walls, before you paint the woodwork and other details.

Using a Roller or Paint Pad

Rollers can make short work of covering large surfaces, after you have cut in. First, tip a little paint into the reservoir of the tray, taking care not to fill it above the area where the textured section begins. Then push the roller across the textured section of the tray and glide it over the paint surface. Do not submerge it in the paint or you could overload it. Next, move the roller backwards and forwards slowly over the textured section to distribute the paint evenly over the roller sleeve.

Apply the paint on the surface by rolling it up and down and then lay off the freshly applied paint using gentle strokes of your roller.

Using a paint pad is quite similar to using a roller. Pour some paint into the tray first and dip the pad into the reservoir before working the excess off on the textured area. Apply the paint to the wall in an up-and-down motion. Pads are popular because they create a very even coat that means that laying off the paint should be unnecessary.

SPEEDY COVER
Using a roller allows you to cover large areas in a short space of time (*below*).

ADD LENGTH
Make light work of painting ceilings by using an extension pole on your roller (*right*).

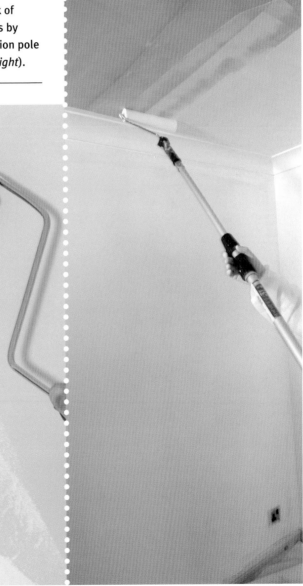

Ceilings

Painting a ceiling is best tackled using a roller with an extension pole (see previous page). Depending on how high your ceilings are, you might prefer to create a platform by securing a scaffolding plank to two stepladders. However, you may find it easier to simply stand on a sturdy chair that you simply move about the room as you are cutting in each section of the edge.

There's a good chance that some paint might drip or spatter into your eyes if you are using a roller on the ceiling, so it is definitely advisable to wear some goggles as a precautionary measure.

Cut in first, using a thin brush, then roll the paint in strips parallel to the window wall, working away from the light, and laying off each area before you reload the roller.

Walls

Once you have cut in the walls, you can use a roller to apply paint in vertical sections. You can use an extension pole to help you avoid bending to paint the lower sections or reaching backwards to paint the higher area. Special long-handled rollers are available for painting tricky areas such as behind radiators. If you are working in a more complex area such as a

hallway, it is best to work from the top down. Start with the ceilings, then continue with the walls of the landing and stairwell, starting at the top. Next paint the woodwork, leaving the stair treads, banisters, handrail and newel posts until last.

Doors

Very simple flush doors can be painted with a roller, working in sections from the top down, and taking care to lay off the paint and merge the joins between each section as you work. However, the majority of doors in the UK are panelled and painting them requires a rather more complex process.

do it PAINT A PANELLED DOOR

This is easy if you work in a set order.

1 Remove the door furniture. Simply unscrew, unless it is painted **A**.

2 Fill any dents or cracks with filler, leave to dry, then sand **B**.

3 Starting at the top, first paint the door frame, the mouldings and the opening edge of the door with a narrow brush **C**.

4 Paint the detailed areas around each panel of the door **D**.

5 Next fill in the door panels, one by one, working from the top down **E**.

6 You can then use a small roller on the larger flat sections of the door **F**.

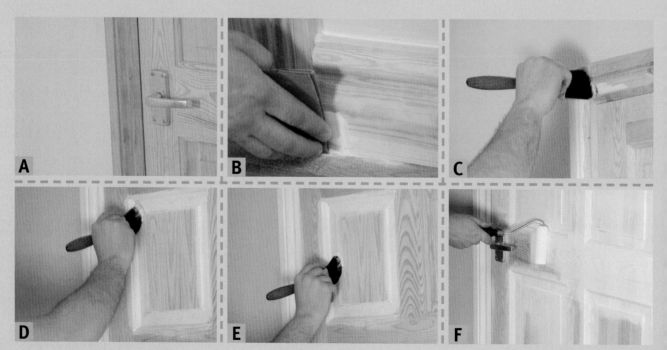

PROTECTING GLASS

Using masking tape on windows can save you hours of paint scraping later on, but be sure to use it away from direct sunlight and do not leave in place. An alternative is a painting shield (see page 110).

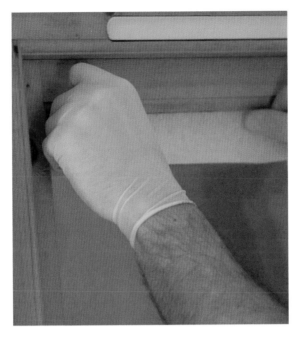

Windows

Always try to paint windows first thing in the morning, so that they will be dry enough to close before you go to bed. For security reasons, plan ahead so that you can be at home all day while the windows are drying.

toptip*

As soon as the paint is touch-dry, remove the masking tape from the window. This will avoid pulling off flakes of paint.

---

doit PAINT A WOODEN WINDOW SILL

1 First fill any cracks with a wood filler designed for exterior use **A**.

2 Sand the sill to remove loose old paint and create a level surface. This is much easier if you wrap paper around a sanding block **B**.

3 Use a medium width – 2in (5cm) – brush to apply a layer of undercoat **C**.

4 When the paint is dry, sand again to remove any minor imperfections **D**.

5 Apply a coat of gloss paint, working in the direction of the wood grain **E**.

6 If painted properly, wooden windows can look good for many years **F**.

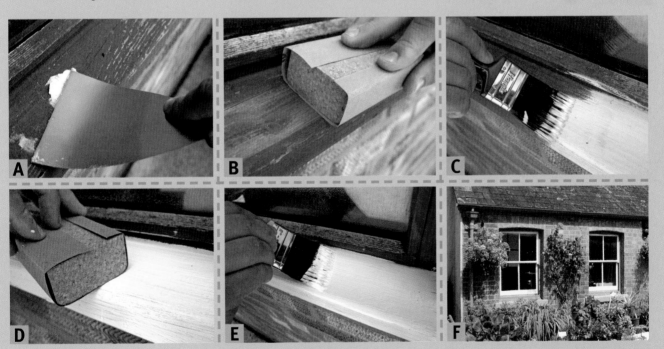

WORTH THE TROUBLE
Sash windows demand
a lot of work, but if well
painted, are a delightful
feature (*below*). For
protecting the glass
when painting a window
frame, a shield is a
useful alternative to
masking tape (*right*).

Sash Windows

These should be painted in two stages.
First lower the outer sash as far as you can
and then raise the outer sash to around 6in
(15cm) from the pulley head. Paint as much
of the outer sash as you can, the bottom
edge of the inner sash and the tops of
the pulley stiles. Once this has completely
dried, you can push the windows to
the reverse position to paint the rest of
the woodwork.

Casement Windows

The easiest option is to start nearest the
glass with the rebates, then proceed up to
the glazing bars themselves. If the bars are
narrow, use a thin brush, such as your cutting
in brush, at an angle to get into the corners.

Floors

Painting or staining floors is considerably
cheaper than buying carpets and underlay
and can be used to create a hard-wearing
and attractive surface. Before you begin
you need a smooth surface to work on,
and it is important to sort out any loose
or damaged boards first, then strip off
any old varnish or polish. You can use oil-
based paints – either gloss or matt – on
wooden floors, but remember to use primer
or undercoat if necessary. You can also
use emulsion on your floorboards, but it
will need to be covered with a layer of
protective polyurethane varnish.

toptip*****

When painting a floor, start with the area
furthest from the door and then work
backwards towards the door, so you can
leave the room while the paint is drying.
If there are other people who are likely to
use the room, ensure that they are aware
you are painting the floor – this is especially
important if there is more than one doorway
into the room.

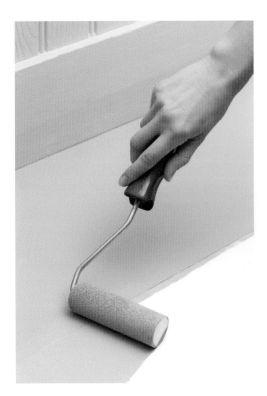

THE HARDER-WEARING OPTION
You can buy specialist floor paints which are very hard-wearing (*left*).

AT THE END OF THE DAY
Once work is completed on a room, take time to decant some of each paint colour into a clearly labelled glass jar and clean your brushes thoroughly ready for next time (*below*).

When the job is done

When you have finished decorating a room, it is tempting to bundle your paint and tools away and forget all about them. However, paintwork can get scuffed or chipped and, if you take a few minutes to store some of your paint for touch-ups, a time will probably come when you will be very glad that you have done that.

You don't have to have lots of old tins hanging around getting rusty – simply decant the remainder of each tin into a clean jam jar with a screw-top lid and screw the lid on firmly. Then – and this is vital – label the jar with the name of the colour, the room you have used it in, the type of paint, the date you've used it, and store it in a cool, dry place.

If you have more paint left over than you anticipated, and you don't think you'll be able to use it all again, you can pass the remainder on. Sites such as wasteconnect. co.uk or communityrepaint.org recognize that your 'waste paint' is a valuable resource, so do your bit for the environment and your local community by donating your paint to them. Passing it on will also free-up valuable storage space in your home.

✳ Good Practice

✔ Once work is completed on a room, take time to decant some of each paint colour into a clearly labelled glass jar.

✔ Store the paint in a cool, dry place.

✔ Clean your brushes thoroughly ready for next time.

✔ If you have too much paint left over to store conveniently, try and recycle it, either through an Internet site, or by donating it to the local community.

CAUTION TAKE PROTECTIVE MEASURES

Doing any DIY can be dangerous, and many people are killed or injured each year when they embark on jobs around the home without taking the proper precautions. Follow these easy pointers to decorating safely:

■ Carefully plan the job before you start work, and leave yourself enough time to finish it properly. Rushing through your work, or working when you are tired, can cause accidents. Know your limitations and consult a professional if you are unsure.

■ To speed up the job, it's a good idea to enlist help with your DIY work – even if it means having a friend around to keep you cheerful.

■ Work in daylight where possible, or ensure you have a bright source of electric light.

■ Make a point of always using the correct tools for the job.

Remember that good quality tools are the best choice in more ways than one, and the right equipment is the key to a successful job.

■ Read the instructions carefully and make sure you know how to operate any power tools you plan to use; either use cordless options, or ensure that the lead is long enough for you to use safely.

■ Never underestimate the importance of safety equipment. Always wear protective clothing such as safety goggles and a dust mask when working with potentially hazardous materials such as spray paint. Invest in a heavy-duty pair of chemical-resistant gloves to wear when handling caustic solutions such as paint stripper.

■ Remember to wear a mask when working in a dusty environment and use ear plugs when operating noisy machinery.

■ Open doors and windows to keep the room well ventilated when painting, or using any material that generates toxic fumes or dust.

■ Never smoke, or allow visitors to smoke, while painting or standing close to a freshly painted area.

■ If you are using tools with a blade, get into the habit of always cutting away from you.

■ Never use water to put out a fire in an electrical appliance. Use a carbon dioxide or halon extinguisher to smother the fire.

■ Always switch off the power and remove the fuse or circuit breaker (MCB) first, if you are fixing or checking electrical appliances or connections. Wear rubber-soled shoes when working on electrics.

■ Leave gas and electrical work to a registered professional. They have years of training and will be well worth their fees.

■ Do not wear loose clothing or jewellery, which could get caught in a power tool.

■ If you plan to use a power drill, choose a model that has a plastic non-conducting body. Always unplug the drill before fitting parts and remove the chuck key before switching it on.

■ Read the instructions thoroughly before you use a ladder – their misuse is the number one cause of decorating accidents in the UK. Always erect the ladder according to the manufacturer's instructions and avoid leaning to one side, as you could lose balance.

■ Always store your tools, paint and solvents in a safe place, out of the way of both children and pets.

■ If you are working in an older building and you uncover any blue or grey fibrous material with a powdery surface, then get it checked, as it may be asbestos. Contact experts to remove it for you, and follow their advice on the best way to leave the area in the meantime.

■ Try to work in a logical sequence and clear up as you go along – lots of accidents are caused by tripping over small obstructions.

■ Take regular breaks from your work, especially when undertaking repetitive tasks, such as painting ceilings or stripping wood, which could cause strain on any particular part of your body.

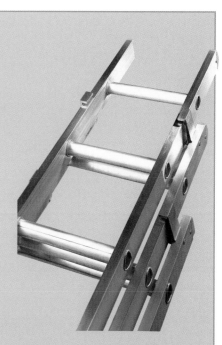

■ Make a point of stopping for a cup of tea from time to time – remember that decorating your home can be good fun!

Decorative Paint Techniques

Stencils

Stencils are effective on walls, ceilings, floors and furniture. They can be used to create your own unique look in a range of rooms, and they are a quick and simple way of enlivening spaces such as a child's bedroom. Before you begin, the walls and surfaces should be prepared thoroughly (see page 56) as any cracks or dents are likely to be made more obvious by the stencil design. Stencils work best on surfaces painted with a matt finish.

A UNIQUE TOUCH

Try to keep your brush almost dry as you stipple paint into the openings of the stencil (*right*). Using stencils enables you to personalize a room in a very short time (*far right*).
Bold, colourful designs are ideal in a child's bedroom (*below*).

✳ Tools of the Trade

It's well worth getting the following equipment together before you begin:

- ✔ Palette
- ✔ Paper towels
- ✔ Ruler
- ✔ Stencil
- ✔ Soft pencil
- ✔ Spirit level
- ✔ Stencil adhesive
- ✔ Stencil brush
- ✔ Stencil paint

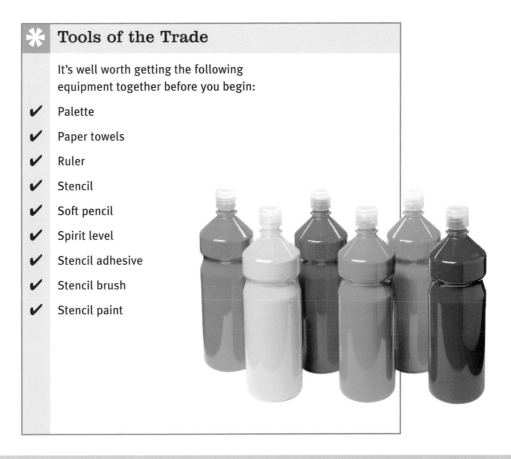

do it STENCILLING

1 It is generally a good idea to start stencilling in the most inconspicuous corner of the room. Use the spirit level and a soft pencil to draw some guidelines, spray a light layer of adhesive to the back of the stencil and then stick it into place.

2 Pour a small amount of paint on the palette and dip just the very tips of the bristles of your stencil brush into the paint. Lay off any excess paint on the paper towel, as you are aiming for a dry brush: if your brush is at all moist with paint, it will seep under the edges of the stencil and blur the edges of the finished design.

3 Use a dabbing motion to stipple paint into the openings. It is better to build the colour up in layers than try to apply a thick coat all in one go.

4 When you have finished, wash your palette, stencil and brushes with warm, soapy water. When the paint is fully dry, simply peel the stencil from the wall to reveal your design.

ANTIQUE MIRROR
Gold leaf was used on this nineteenth-century mirror frame (*right*).

Gilding

Gilding is a technique that originally involved using incredibly thin sheets of very finely beaten precious metals. It was extremely expensive and therefore only used in churches and the homes of the very wealthy. If you have an expensive item such as an antique mirror or picture frame that needs gilding, it may be worth going to a specialist who will use real gold leaf.

For everyday items, and larger surfaces, however, you will probably find that the opulent appearance offered by metallic paint is much more affordable and easy to achieve.

GO FOR IMPACT
Used carefully, metallic paints can create stunning effects (*below and facing page*).

Metallic Paint

These water-based paints can look stunning on an accent wall, ceiling, or part of a room, and can help you to create a feature. They produce a shimmery effect and are available in a large range of colours – from gold, bronze, copper and silver effects to sparkling blues, purples, pinks, reds and greens. Some may be suitable for exterior use, but check before you buy.

Using a brush or roller, metallics can be applied on primed surfaces in thin coats until you get an even finish – bear in mind that this may require more than two coats.

As they reflect light, metallic paints will show up any imperfections such as dents, bumps or cracks in the wall surface, so always ensure that the surface is smooth.

It can take a little practice to get the hang of applying an even coat but, if you work methodically and carefully, you can achieve impressive results.

do it METALLIC PAINT

1 As metallic paint is expensive, you may prefer to start with a base coat of emulsion in a similar shade.

2 First use a brush to cut in (see page 106). Then, working on small sections at a time, use a roller with a synthetic, short pile sleeve to apply the paint evenly and consistently and in a uniform direction.

3 Make sure your last stroke always goes in one direction, as this aligns all the metallic pigments and helps you to avoid overlap marks and roller marks.

4 When you have finished one small section, paint another strip. Make sure you overlap the first strip so that you're working wet paint onto wet paint. Some metallic paints dry faster than ordinary paint, so try to work in a methodical manner.

Ageing Techniques

Antiquing or 'ageing' is the procedure used to simulate natural wear and tear with the use of paint glazes. You may choose to apply this finish to your walls and floors, or to furniture, built-in cabinets and accessories. The distressed look can make an object more comfortable to live with and help a new item blend in with older surroundings.

The 'shabby chic' effect works well in period and country homes and can be achieved by using a special glaze or varnish on the surface to be covered.

Crackle Glaze

'Crackle glaze' is a special paint you can buy in DIY stores that is applied over the finished surface. As the glaze dries it breaks up (or cracks) to reveal the colour underneath. Surfaces need to be clean and dry and free of dirt, oil, or wax before antiquing. Proprietary glazes are inexpensive, and you simply use a brush to paint them over the desired area. They often dry very quickly, so it is best to apply them on a cool day, or turn the heating down if you are using them in winter.

'DISTRESSING'
This chair (*above right*) has been colour-washed, to blend in with the Roman-style bathroom. Crackle glaze is a very attractive way of 'antiquing' a surface (*right*).

Limewash

Although it has become extremely popular in the last decade or so, limewash is actually one of the earliest forms of paint and has been in use for thousands of years. Limewashed surfaces have a unique matt patina and this vapour-permeable paint is ideal on older properties, as it allows walls to breathe.

Limewash is a mixture of calcium hydroxide and natural colour pigments in water, and as it dries it absorbs carbon dioxide from the air.

This reaction produces tiny, light-reflective crystals, which give limewashed walls their unmistakable 'glowing' finish. Lime is a caustic product and so when applying limewash, you should always wear safety goggles or glasses and chemical-resistant gloves.

ADD CHARACTER

Limewash is ideal for older properties and offers a unique finish (*below*).

Limewash can take up to five days or so to dry out so, if you are planning to work on the exterior of your house, try to do it in a period of fine weather.

USE INSIDE OR OUTSIDE
Limewash can be used on interior walls (*above left and right*) and exterior walls (*right*).

do it LIMEWASH A WALL

1 Before applying limewash, ensure your walls are fully prepared (see page 56). Limewash works best on absorbent surfaces. It sticks well to lime plasters and renders, stone, brick and similar materials, but does not adhere so well to modern materials and finishes. So, in some circumstances, it may be necessary to add casein, tallow or raw linseed oil to the limewash to help it stick to the walls.

2 Wash down the entire surface using a soft scrubbing brush to ensure that any dust is removed. All surfaces to be limewashed should be moistened with clean, cold water and left until the surface is damp but not wet.

3 Use a large, soft brush to apply limewash – such as a dustpan brush with soft bristles – and, rather than painting the wall, use a circular motion to almost scrub it into the surface.

4 Ensure that the limewash is worked well into the surface and spread as far as possible – bearing in mind that you should aim for a very thin layer. Finish off with vertical strokes.

5 Limewash changes colour as it dries, becoming more rich and vibrant, so don't panic if it looks a little pale and wishy-washy at first. You can apply further layers once the wash is completely dry (ideally after around five days).

Limewash is a 'breathable' covering, which makes it ideal for use on the exterior of older buildings, such as country cottages.

STUNNING COLOUR
As limewash dries out
the colours intensify,
leaving a rich, vibrant
finish (*left*).

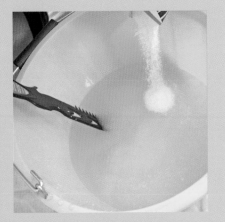

4 Using Wallpaper

Wallpaper can transform a room, enabling you to achieve a great variety of looks, from simple country floral to dark and sumptuous.

Before You Begin

PLENTY OF CHOICE
Available in an incredible variety of patterns, wallpaper is a unique decorating tool (*above*).

In the past, wallpaper was only used in the most affluent of homes and was considered to be a sign of great elegance and wealth. Now it is far more affordable and easy to use, and you can choose from a huge range of different wallpapers today.

These include varietiess that you stick to the wall using proprietary paste, pre-pasted wallpaper and there is even self-adhesive wallpaper, with a removable backing that you simply have to peel off, before you affix the paper to the wall.

Measuring Up

Before you go shopping to choose wallpaper, measure the room carefully. Although you may be surprised at how much space in the room is taken up with features such as doorways, windows and fireplaces, remember that you'll need to paper above and around them, so unless you are using a very plain design, it is best to simply ignore doors and windows in your calculations. Exceptions to this are large French doors, or floor-to-ceiling windows.

The chart below is a useful guide but, as a general rule, simply multiply the number of yards (or metres) around the room by the height of the walls to help you to calculate how many rolls you need. Standard rolls are 33ft (10.05m) long and 1ft 9in (53cm) wide, but remember to check each roll before you buy as they can vary.

If you have an old roll of wallpaper from a previous job, you can use this to get an accurate assessment of the number of 'drops'

Most DIY stores have charts to help you work out how much wallpaper you will need, but always double check, if in doubt. If you're buying repeat patterns you need to allow for wastage, as you will be matching the lengths before you hang them.

If the wallpaper has a large repeat motif, you will need more rolls to allow for wastage as you line up each drop.

you will need to paper the entire room. You can walk around the room holding the paper roll against the wall and use a pencil to mark how many roll widths you will need to complete the room. Measure the height and work out how many drops you will get from the average roll.

Divide the number of drops into the roll length, and you will have the number of drops you will get from each roll. Work out how many drops you need to complete the job, allowing for wastage, and you will then have the number of rolls you need.

Ask in the shop if they will let you return any rolls you do not use, provided that they are unopened and you keep your receipt. Most DIY stores will let you do this as long as you return the rolls in a reasonable time frame. Then you can err on the side of caution and buy an extra roll or two, so that you are covered for wastage and any accidental damage that may occur.

HOW MANY ROLLS DO YOU NEED TO PAPER WALLS?

Wall height	Distance around room, including doors and windows							
	33ft (10m)	39ft (12m)	46ft (14m)	52ft (16m)	59ft (18m)	66ft (20m)	72ft (22m)	79ft (24m)
7–7ft 6in (2.2–2.3m)	5	5	6	7	8	9	10	11
7ft 6in –8ft (2.3–2.4m)	5	6	7	8	9	10	10	11
8ft–8ft 6in (2.4–2.6m)	5	6	7	9	10	11	12	13
8ft 6in–9ft (2.6–2.7m)	5	6	7	9	10	11	12	13
9ft–9ft 6in (2.7–2.9m)	6	7	8	9	10	12	12	14

The finest quality
wallpaper is hand-
printed by artisans.
It has a unique finish
and a price tag to
match (*above*).

Choosing a 'Look'

Think about the look you wish to achieve
in the room, and consider whether it is
better to wallpaper the whole room, or just
a specific area, such as the wall around
the fireplace, for example. If you are new
to hanging wallpaper, it's wise to start
out with a small print so that slight mis-
matches will be less noticeable.

Wall coverings increase visual interest
by adding pattern, texture and accent
colour to a room. They can be used
dramatically to define a room style. For
example, a bold abstract print immediately
establishes a contemporary style, while a
small floral design will suggest a more
traditional or country theme.

toptip*

Wallpaper is printed
in batches, and it's
important to buy rolls
with the same batch
number to ensure
that they will all be
exactly the same
colour. Separate
batches can have
small differences in
colour or finish that
can stick out like a
sore thumb when
placed next to each
other on your wall.

Wallpaper Patterns

The size and style of the pattern you choose can make a huge difference to the look of a room. The colours you select have an impact in their own right, but patterns can also contribute to the appearance of more or less space.

Before you choose, assess the feel of a room and what you want to achieve. If it is awkwardly shaped, there are lots of visual cues you can employ to minimize this. For example, if a room is long and thin, you can make it seem more in proportion by using vertical striped wallpaper on the walls and painting the ceiling white.

SPOILT FOR CHOICE
The style, size of pattern and colour of your wallpaper can determine the feel of a room.

✳ Tricks of the Trade

✔ Horizontal stripes can make a room seem wider **A**.

✔ Large, vertical patterns on walls and stripes can make a room seem taller **B**.

✔ Dark shades and big, busy patterns can make a room seem smaller and more intimate **C**.

✔ Small prints or light colours can make a room seem more spacious **D**.

A

B

C

D

Types of Wallpaper

SIZE MATTERS

There is a huge array of different papers to choose from. If you are using a bold pattern, you may choose to use it on a feature wall and paint the other walls in a toning colour (*left*). Rolls of hand-printed wallpaper are available from specialist suppliers (*below*).

Take great care to avoid splashing paste on the front of the foil paper. Pre-pasted versions of foil wallpaper are also available, but can be difficult to hang, so they are not recommended for beginners.

HAND-PRINTED WALLPAPER

Available in hand-blocked, screen-printed or surface-printed options. Companies such as Cole & Son have been manufacturing wallpaper since the 1800s and their papers are used in Buckingham Palace, the Houses of Parliament and Brighton Pavilion. The hand-carved wooden blocks Cole & Son use include designs by Augustus Pugin, William Morris and Charles Voysey.

12 Types of Wallpaper

ANAGLYPTA

A white, thick relief paper with an embossed pattern. Anaglypta is usually painted over with emulsion, or resin-based paint. It is an ideal covering for a poor surface, as it disguises many lumps and bumps. The decoration can be changed with extra coats of paint.

It is hard-wearing, available in fine textures and many colours and can be wiped clean. However, it tends to be quite thin, so is unsuitable for poor wall surfaces, as the uneven areas will show through. The metallic coating can conduct electricity, so should not be tucked behind light switch or plug covers when hanging.

FLOCK WALLPAPER This has a fine-pile synthetic or natural embossed surface, glued to backing paper. It often gives a velvet texture and is rich in colour. It is one of the more expensive wallpapers, and a difficult paper to hang, as any paste touching the surface will ruin the pile. If it becomes stained, it can be carefully sponged, or can be gently brushed to remove surface dust.

FOIL WALLPAPER This has a metallic plastic film on a paper backing, and is an option is well worth considering for darker areas because the shiny surface helps to reflect light.

Hand-blocking is a technique that requires immense skill and a long apprenticeship. The effect of hand-blocking is a heavy build-up of colour, providing a special depth and graining. Another advantage of block printing is that large repeat sizes of up to 72in (183cm) are available so, if you have a sizeable room to decorate – and a sizeable budget to go with it – they are a very good option, although they tend not be as hard-wearing as machine-printed options, as their colours are not as fast and they can tear when wet. They can, however, be lightly wiped if dirty but cannot be washed, so are unsuitable for busy areas. Delicate patterns are also more difficult to match, and the accuracy of the pattern may not be as uniform as machine-printed papers, but this is often considered to be part of their charm. Hand-printed papers are not recommended for areas where there is a build-up of steam or condensation.

LINCRUSTAS A textured option, that was very popular in late Victorian and Edwardian homes. Lincrustas are a good choice for staircases, due to their durable, easy-to-clean surface. The raised pattern is a solid film of linseed oil and fillers, that is fused onto a backing paper.

LINING PAPER A plain, flat option that can be used before wallpaper on uneven or painted surfaces. Papering a ceiling is much harder than papering walls, but you may find it is a relatively easy way to cover cracks. Lining paper is available in different thicknesses.

NOVAMURA is made from foamed polyethylene. It is available in a wide range of patterns and colours. It is relatively easy to hang and very light to manoeuvre as there is no paper content. The surface of novamura is warm to the touch and often resembles fabric.

Novamura is useful for high-traffic areas, because light knocks are unlikely to damage the surface. It is a good choice in bathrooms and kitchens as steam does not damage it.

POLYSTYRENE This sheeting can be used to line walls before papering. It can help to make a wall feel warm to the touch, and has good insulating qualities. However, it dents easily if knocked by furniture and is, therefore, unsuitable for busy areas, such as hallways and dining rooms.

MACHINE-PRINTED WALLPAPER The most readily available option, and is therefore quite reasonably priced, and offers a huge variety of choices.

SUGALYPTA This is a stronger version of Anaglypta. Cotton fibres are used in place of wood pulp, which allows a deeper embossed pattern. It is then painted over.

VINYL WALLPAPER This has the design printed on a layer of vinyl. It has a fine paper backing and gives an easy-to-wipe surface.

Expanded vinyl has a texture similar to a heavy embossed paper, but requires less paste for hanging. It has a very durable surface, which can even be lightly scrubbed, making it particularly suitable for kitchens and bathrooms.

WASHABLE WALLPAPER This is ordinary printed wallpaper that is either coated with a thin glaze of polyvinyl acetate (PVA), or is printed with water-resistant inks. It provides an easy-to-wipe surface and is particularly suitable for kitchens and bathrooms.

WOODCHIP PAPER A relatively inexpensive option for covering walls. It is a plain paper with a textured oatmeal surface, made by impregnating the pulp with sawdust and woodchip during its manufacture. It then needs to be painted and can be covered in a variety of coloured emulsions. Woodchip can be very tricky to strip, as the chips of wood have a habit of sticking to the wall.

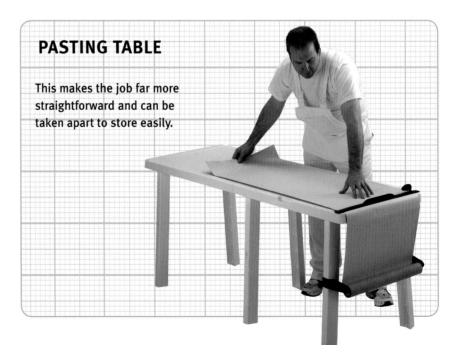

PASTING TABLE

This makes the job far more straightforward and can be taken apart to store easily.

Papering a Wall

✴ Basic tools and equipment

- ✔ Craft knife
- ✔ Bucket
- ✔ Extending steel tape
- ✔ Clean sponge
- ✔ Wallpaper shears
- ✔ Seam roller
- ✔ Hanging brush
- ✔ Pasting brush
- ✔ Straight edge
- ✔ Chalk canister and plumbline

It's also well worth buying or borrowing a pasting table. They fold flat when not in use so won't take up too much room in your tool shed or garage. If you have a large kitchen or dining table, you may prefer to use this instead, but cover it with a heavy-duty polyethelene sheet first to protect it.

First you need to remove old wallpaper (see page 56) and ensure you have a clean and even surface to work on. Remove items such as curtain tracks and ensure you put dust sheets on the floor. If there are areas of the room such as windows and doors that you need to paint, it is wise to do this before you begin wallpapering. If you are going to paper the ceiling, do this first before you begin the walls.

top tips ✴

There are two things to bear in mind if you are planning to wallpaper a newly built house. Firstly, plaster can take around six months to dry out thoroughly enough to be wallpapered over. Secondly, new plasterboard surfaces should be sealed with a coat of emulsion before you hang any wall coverings.

Tie a thick piece of taut string across the top of your plastic bucket. This provides a handy place to wipe off excess paste from your brush.

USE A DRY BRUSH
Dust the walls with a dry brush before you commence work (*below*).

CHOICE OF PASTE
Cellulose paste is the best choice for light wallpapers as it does not stain. You can buy ready-mixed paste in a tub (*below*).

1 Carefully measure the length required (normally the height of the wall) and cut from the roll, allowing an extra 2in (5cm) or so at top and bottom for final trimming. To start with, only cut one length at a time **A**.

2 Ensure the pattern is the right way up and never assume that the outside end of the roll is the top, as it is not always the case. Mark the back of the paper with a 'T' at the top, to avoid confusion later on.

3 Consider where you will start hanging. For boldly patterned wallpapers it's helpful to choose a focal point such as a chimney breast, or the main wall you'll look at when you are sitting in the room. Hang from the centre of that wall, so that the design looks balanced. If you have a plainer design, it is often easier to simply start in a corner, usually behind the door **B**.

4 With a bold design, always cut the first length so that when it is hung and finally trimmed top and bottom, there will be a complete motif at the top of the wall **C**.

5 Before cutting the next lengths, always ensure that the pattern matches up with previous ones. Remember that you will be using more wall coverings if the design is large or has a big repeat. It's a good idea to keep tidying up as you work but don't throw your offcuts away – they may come in useful for small areas, such as above doors or around windows.

6 Always use the paste that is recommended on the roll label or leaflet, as some contain a fungicide that's necessary for vinyls and washable papers. Follow the paste

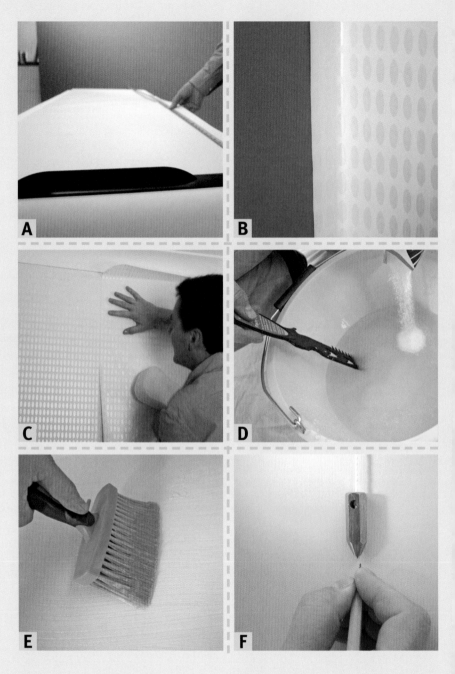

manufacturer's instructions carefully, especially when mixing, so that you achieve the correct consistency **D**.

7 Try to avoid getting paste on the front surface of the paper but, if you do, remove it carefully with a damp sponge. Check the pasting table regularly for spills and keep your hands clean and dry at all times **E**.

8 When the paste is properly mixed, lay the paper face down on the table. Starting from the top, brush the paste down the length and out towards the edges, herringbone fashion, so that it evenly covers the surface. Never pull the brush back across the edge of the paper, as you can end up with paste on the front of the paper.

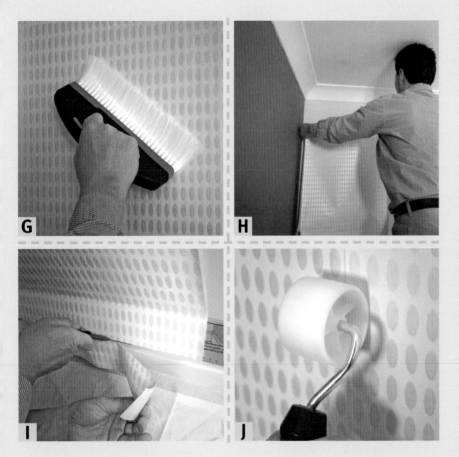

14 Once the paper has soaked, check which is the top of the wallcovering (ideally you will have used a soft pencil to mark it on the back, as mentioned in step 2, before pasting), and carry it to the wall.

15 Holding the top of the length, carefully open the top fold and lightly stick the top half of the length to the wall. Allow about 2in (5cm) at the top of the wall for trimming off, and slide the wall covering exactly into position. Smooth down the middle with a paperhanger's brush, ensuring a good butt joint and pattern match, then work out towards the edges, removing air bubbles **H**.

16 Open the bottom fold and continue to smooth the paper down to the skirting. Carefully run the back of the scissors along the angle of the ceiling and the wall at the top, and the skirting at the bottom, to make an impression where the wall covering has to be cut off.

17 Gently pull the length away, trim off the excess with scissors, and brush back into place **I**.

18 Use a damp sponge to carefully wipe surplus paste from the surface of the paper and the skirting and ceiling, to avoid it marking those surfaces when it dries. Wash your sponge frequently, and use a roller to press down the seams as you go along **J**.

9 Fold the pasted length inwards, bottom to middle and top to middle. To ensure the edges do not curl back and dry out, the folded length can be loosely rolled to hold it together during the soaking period. For very long lengths, fold like a concertina.

10 Once pasted, all wall coverings need to 'soak' for a period of time before hanging. This allows the moisture to be absorbed and the paper to fully expand. Always read the manufacturer's instructions on the label.

11 Few walls are truly square, or perfectly vertical. To overcome this, and to avoid your pattern going askew, always mark a vertical pencil line against a plumb

line or long spirit level. (You can make your own plumb line with a weight attached to a thin string) **F**.

12 Allow the plumb to swing freely until it is at rest before putting your pencil mark down the wall behind the string. The plumb line should be about 1in (25mm) less than the width of the wall covering away from the starting point.

13 Don't hang on the line, but just leave it showing by about ¹/₄ in (5mm) and hang parallel with it. Next, smooth down and brush back the length away from the line and into the corner, going round the corner by about 10in (25cm) **G**.

doit AVOIDING BLISTERS IN THE PAPER

If blisters appear as the wall covering lengths start to dry out, this is usually because there are some air pockets underneath. If the bubbles persist, it could mean that the wall covering has not had time to absorb sufficient moisture from the paste – indicating that the lengths need to be left longer after pasting so that they become 'limp' before hanging.

After you wet the paper with paste, the fibres will start to expand. If the wall covering is put onto the wall before this has finished, the fibres will continue to expand, causing blisters to form.

Sometimes these flatten out after the wall covering has dried out – but not always.

Other causes of blisters are too thin a paste, giving either a lack of adhesion in places or lack of penetration into the wall covering. Similarly if your pasting is patchy, it will allow areas of wall covering to be missed and left dry. On the other hand, if you make the paste too thick or overload the wall covering with paste, you can cause a range of problems such as blistering, creasing, stretching and flattening of the emboss.

1 If you spot a blister in the paper, ease the paper away from the wall and then brush it down again, expelling the air as you do so **A**.

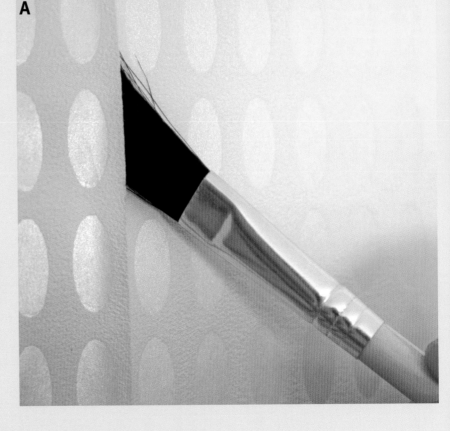

A

doit SWITCHES AND SOCKETS

1 First, turn the electricity off at the mains, then smooth the wallpaper down very gently over the fitting, and use a scalpel to pierce the paper, and make diagonal cuts from the centre to about 1in (2.5cm) beyond each corner **A**.

2 Press the wallpaper firmly around the edge of the fitting, lightly mark the outline and trim away the surplus **B**.

Some decorators prefer to slightly unscrew the fitting so that the wallpaper can be tucked just behind its edges. Particular care is needed with ready-pasted wallcoverings, because they usually carry a lot of water. Similarly, take care with metallic foil wallpapers, as the foil layer could act as a conductor.

CAUTION ELECTRICAL SAFETY

■ Be very careful when applying wallpaper over, under or around electrical switches, sockets and similar items. Always turn the supply off at the mains first.

doit PAPERING CORNERS

Never wrap a full width wall covering round an inside corner – you get a much better finish if you do it in two pieces.

1 First measure the distance from the edge of the last piece you hung to the corner. Do this at several points between the ceiling and skirting to find the maximum distance **A**.

2 Cut a length of wall covering so that it is about 1in (2.5cm) wider than this measurement, paste it and hang with the extra 1in (2.5cm) overlapping round the corner on to the next wall. Where corners are not accurately plastered, you must be more generous with the overlap **B**.

3 Take the remainder of the length and paste it. Measure it and mark a vertical guideline on the next wall, a little more than its width out from the corner **C**.

4 Then take the second length and hang it alongside the vertical line and perfectly parallel to it, brushing back into the corner and overlapping the 1in (2.5cm) which has already been carried round **D**.

5 If you have patterned wallpaper, match it as well as you can, although a slight mismatch in the corner is not normally too obvious. **E**.

6 To paper outside corners, follow the same technique, although you should allow a wrap-round of at least 2in (5cm) **F**.

toptip*

Thicker papers, such as vinyl, can be difficult to stick down along the overlap. In this case, slice through the two thicknesses after overlapping, and remove the surplus pieces from underneath, which will give you a perfect butt joint. When slicing through, use a good straight-edge and a very sharp knife; cut at a low angle – and take great care.

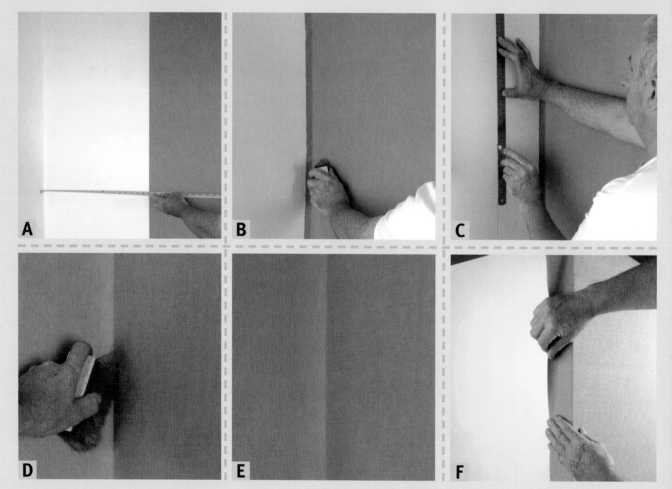

A B C

D E F

do it PAPERING AROUND DOORS AND WINDOWS

1 Align the wallpaper to the last drop of paper. Do NOT align the paper to the door frame **A**.

2 Smooth the paper down carefully, all over, using a wallpapering brush **B**.

3 Run your fingers down the wallpaper, to push it neatly into the architrave **C**.

4 Run a knife down the line where the paper meets the architrave, and gently pull the waste away while the adhesive is still wet **D**.

5 Infill over the top of the door or window with a short strip of paper, but ensure that it is long enough to allow an overlap top and bottom, for trimming afterwards **E**.

6 The completed job **F**.

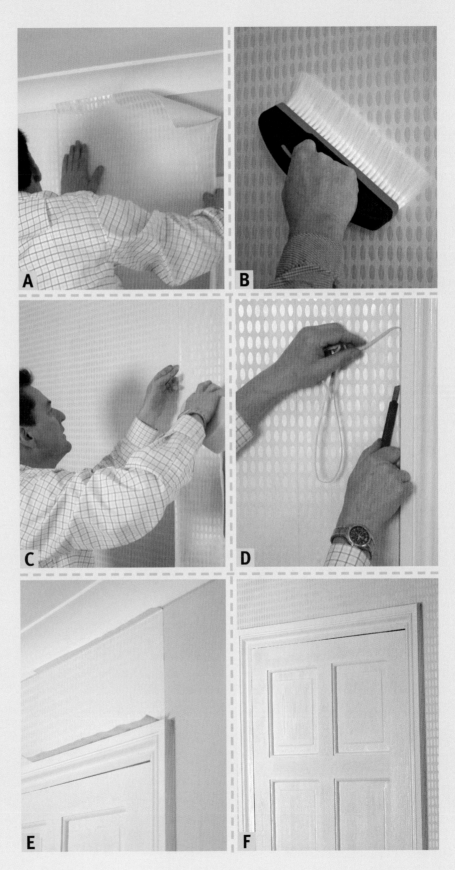

5

Interior Updates

Once your home is decorated to your taste,

you will want to keep it looking good in years

to come. Here are some ideas to inspire you.

Ringing the Changes

If you have prepared your surfaces well before you began to decorate, then your handiwork should look good for years to come. However, small cracks can appear, paintwork can be scraped or scuffed and you are bound to need a few simple touch-ups from time to time.

Cracks can be filled with decorator's caulk and then painted over, while small dents are best repaired with ready-mixed filler, before being sanded and painted over (see page 58).

toptip*

Paint tends to change colour as it dries, often getting a shade lighter, so don't be alarmed if the colour doesn't quite match right away – as long as you labelled the jars clearly (see page 111), you can't go far wrong.

DEALING WITH DENTS

If small dents appear on your walls, apply a little filler, leave it to dry and then sand it smooth before you paint it (*below*).

doit MINOR TOUCH-UPS

1 First stir the paint very thoroughly as it may have settled during storage **A**.

2 Using a small brush, paint over the repair area. Avoid overloading the brush with paint, or you may get drips **B**.

3 Feather the edges into the surrounding wall with a nearly dry roller, by rolling from the centre outwards with numerous light strokes. Lift the roller off the surface as you roll **C**.

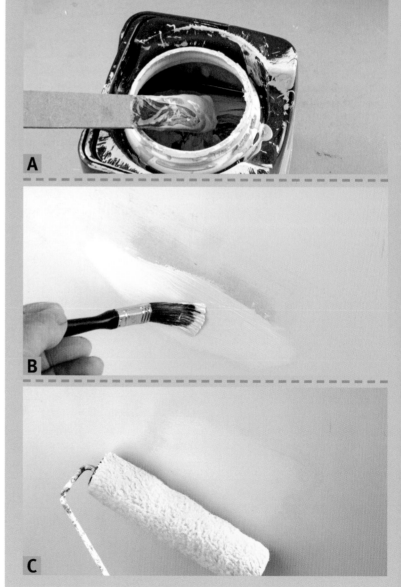

A

B

C

Revamp Your Decor

It is surprising how just a few small touches can make a big difference to the way a room looks. If your decor is looking a little tired, or you simply fancy a change, then some of the following options may be worth trying.

Curtains or Blinds?

Consider swapping your curtains for a blind, if you want to make the room look more contemporary and streamlined. Alternatively, if you have a blind in the window now, think about how it would look with curtains – they can give a room a cosy feel and their insulating properties may well be very welcome in winter.

INSTANT MAKEOVER
Your choice of curtains or blinds can have a massive impact on the atmosphere of the room (*below*).

toptip*

Remember that paint and wallpaper are relatively inexpensive, so you can change your mind about certain aspects of a colour scheme quite often and simply buy new paint when you want to refresh the look of a room. However, soft furnishings such as curtains, sofa covers and carpets all represent much more of an investment, so you may prefer to choose neutral options that you can comfortably predict will look good in a range of settings and backdrops.

Shed Some Light

If a room is a little on the dark side, and you just have a single pendant light in the middle of the room, it is worth investing in a lamp or two, whether wall lights, recessed spotlights or table lamps.

The lighting you choose can make a huge impact: light rooms feel larger and more welcoming and the addition of some lamps will allow you to create a very different ambience.

ADD ATMOSPHERE
A few strategically placed lights can change the whole atmosphere of your rooms (*right*).

Tricks of the Trade

The addition of well-placed mirrors is a decorating trick that has been used to make rooms feel larger and lighter for centuries. Traditionally, mirrors were placed over fireplaces, where they would help to reflect some of the light from the fire around the room. Positioning a mirror opposite a window is another good way to increase the feeling of light and space.

ON REFLECTION
Mirrors are especially effective when placed in a spot that reflects light from the main fitting (*below*).

GET FRESH

A well-chosen houseplant or two will immediately make a room feel more inviting (*below*).

Add Houseplants or Flowers

Adding some lush green houseplants, a small tree or a fresh bunch of flowers can also give a room a more inviting atmosphere. If using plants, place them in pots with a saucer underneath to protect the surfaces you leave them on.

Easy options for the less green-fingered include spider plants and peace lilies. The latter are simple to look after, as they droop when they need to be watered – a visible reminder that it is hard to miss.

Keep it Tidy

One of the best ways to improve the look of a room is to tidy away any clutter: clear surfaces on display make a room look orderly and balanced, and create far more relaxed and pleasant surroundings.

The key to keeping rooms clear is to have plenty of storage. Once everything has an assigned space, it is much easier to get into the habit of putting things away.

CLEAR A SPACE
If the tops of desks or shelves are on show, it instantly makes a room look organized and welcoming (*below*).

Reposition the Furniture

Try repositioning the furniture (get a friend to help if it is bulky or heavy) and seeing the impact this has on the overall look. If the room is small, consider removing any items that you don't normally use, or replacing them with dual-purpose items, such as a coffee table that doubles up as a storage chest. In a very large room it can be useful to delineate the space by grouping pieces such as chairs and a table together in smaller areas.

Repeat a Theme

A favourite trick of interior designers is to repeat a certain theme throughout a room. You may have a sofa in a particular colour, for example, so you could consider placing a rug, cushions or a wall-hanging in this shade at the other side of the room. This gives a balanced and unified look.

COLOUR COORDINATE
Create a unified look in your bathroom by investing in some towels that perfectly match the colour of your walls (*right*).

Review the Floor

If your carpet is looking worse for wear, then consider having it professionally cleaned. Alternatively, you could replace it with sanded or painted floorboards, with or without a rug to break up the surface. Alternatively, if you have a wooden floor and noisy children or pets, you may prefer to cover the floor with carpet, which has great sound-insulating properties, and can make a room feel far more cosy.

REPLACE A CARPET
If your carpet is old and tatty, consider changing to floorboards and a well-placed rug or two (*below*).

ADD BALANCE
Symmetrical schemes are very effective, but try to include the odd detail that is offset for extra interest (*below*).

Talk it Over

When you become familiar with a room, it can be difficult to be objective about potential improvements. If in doubt, ask a friend or relative for their suggestions. Often just talking things over helps you to clarify new ideas.

Weigh it Up

We tend to find symmetry very pleasing to the eye. Bear this in mind when positioning pictures, ornaments, furniture and accessories in a room. If you are shopping for a new vase or pot plant, for example, consider buying two.

Types of Blinds and Shutters

If lovely windows are a feature of your home, consider enhancing their looks with stylish blinds or shutters.

6

BLACKOUT ROLLER BLINDS are made from densely woven fabric, which really helps to reduce the amount of light entering a room. They are especially useful in the bedroom for anyone who works at night and needs to sleep during the day. They are also a boon for light sleepers, south-facing bedrooms, or rooms near an external source of artificial light. They can be used behind curtains, or you may prefer to use special blackout curtain linings.

Use them in:
Bedrooms or nurseries.

ROLLER BLINDS are made from fabric which has been specially treated or stiffened, so they remain in place even when a window is open and a breeze blowing through. They are operated by a spring mechanism or beaded side controls. Depending on the pattern of the fabric and the style of the bottom edge, they can be very subtle and discreet, or you can use them to make a bold statement. You can buy or make decorative pulls to enhance your room scheme.

Use them in:
Bedrooms, kitchens, bathrooms and living rooms.

A SOFT TOUCH
Roman blinds are the ideal choice in a cottage-style conservatory (*below*).

ROMAN BLINDS form soft pleats when raised, and hang flat when lowered. The pleats are kept in place by dowel rods or slats that are sewn into casings on the lining. A cording mechanism attached to the dowel rods or slats on the back of the blind allows it to be raised and lowered. They are a good choice for an area such as a bedroom where you want to create a softer look, and are also ideal in a cottage-style living room.

Use them in:
Bedrooms, sitting rooms, conservatories and kitchens.

SHUTTERS were a popular feature of Georgian homes. Often made of hardwood that would typically have been painted white, hinged shutters were built into the alcoves of each window, so that they could easily be pulled across to offer shade, security and insulation. They can be angled to let light in, but also offer privacy.

Use them in:
The windows of eighteenth-century properties, or newer homes if you want privacy and style. If you have original designs, specialist companies can advise you on their restoration. If the shutters in your home were removed by a previous owner, you can have new designs fitted in a classic style.

BEST OF BOTH WORLDS
Choose shutters that can be angled – then you can see out but people cannot see in (*below*).

VENETIAN BLINDS are made with horizontal slats that can be tilted, raised or lowered to let in as much or as little light as you require. The slats are available in a variety of widths and you can choose designs in light metals such as aluminium, plastic, solid wood or wood-effect material. Man-made materials are ideal if you want a contemporary look. The range of colours and styles is endless.

Use them in:
Home offices, studies, studios, conservatories or other areas where being able to adjust the amount of light in the room is imperative. Wooden blinds can be very effective in reception rooms, especially if the floor or furniture in the rooms is a similar shade. Darker woods have a colonial appeal, making them ideal for Victorian homes.

ADD SOME PRIVACY
Venetian blinds can offer privacy while still allowing light to flood into the room (*right*).

VERTICAL BLINDS are a striking choice but due to their complex structure, they will need to be custom-made to fit your window. They consist of vertical strips that can be tilted or drawn using a simple chain control unit. The strips can be partially tilted to admit more or less light, or pulled back completely on one or both sides.

Use them in:
Home offices, bedrooms and conservatories.

CUTTING EDGE
Vertical blinds make a bold statement and are ideal for stylish modern homes (*below*).

About the Author

Jeannine McAndrew is head of the Homes & Gardens department at Aceville Publications, and has 13 years' experience in writing about interiors, decoration and DIY. She is, therefore, well qualified to write about home decorating.

Her own DIY projects have included renovating three houses and, through doing a couple of hours' work a night on her last home, she managed to double its value in just two years.

Jeannine believes that decorating can – and should – be an enjoyable and creative experience, and is keen to share her tips with others, confident that they will also enjoy rapid – and very often valuable – results, while taking great pleasure from living in the home they have created.

Photographic Acknowledgements

GMC Publications would like to thank the following for the use of their photographs:

Karl Anderson & Soner (Product: Trippo-bord; Designer: Ulla Christianson): p. 39; **Laura Ashley** front cover, top right, pp. 12 (bottom), 14, 15 (top right), 19 (right), 24 (bottom right), 33 (bottom left), 44 (bottom right), 65 (top and bottom), 86 (bottom left), 122, 127 (all), 128 (top right), 138, 149 (right), 151 (top right); **Anthony Bailey** (© GMC Publications Ltd) pp. 23 (top right), 31 (top left), 44 (top left), 50 (top), 66 (bottom left), 67 (x 6), 71 (bottom), 75 (bottom x 4), 76 (left), 79 (top right), 81 (top x 5), 85 (bottom right), 86 (right x 4), 87 (top), 88 (x 3), 89 (top), 105 (middle x 2), 110 (bottom), 111 (right), 116 (top), 136 (x 6); **Bsweden** p. 19 (top left); **Davuka** pp. 74, 83 (all), 142; **Farrow & Ball** pp. 10, 18, 28 (bottom right), 33, 37 (bottom right), 41 (top left), 44 (bottom left), 46 (bottom right), 128 (top left and bottom right); **GAD** pp. 5, 23 (bottom left), 43 (bottom), 46 (top), 54; **Gustavian** pp. 15 (top left and bottom left), 20 (top left and bottom right), 21 (bottom left and bottom right), 31 (bottom left and bottom right); **Iform** p. 36 (bottom left); **www. istockphoto.com** pp. 51, 58, 79 (top left), 99 (bottom), 112 (bottom right), 115 (top right), 118 (bottom), 121, 153; **Marston & Langinger** pp. 9 (bottom), 23 (top left and bottom right), 28 (top), 31 (top right), 33 (bottom right), 35 (middle right), 36 (top), 41 (top right), 47, 90, 144, 148, 149 (left), 150; **Rebecca Mothersole** p. 26 (bottom right x 2), p. 29 (top right x 2); **Nordic Style** pp. 15 (right middle and bottom right), 20 (top right, bottom left and bottom middle), 21 (top right); **Sprossa** p. 21 (top left and middle left); Per Erik Jæger p. 27 (bottom left), 93, 103 (top), 124 (top left and bottom right); **Svenskt Tenn AB** pp. 5 (bottom), 35 (top and bottom), 41 (bottom); **Toast** p. 9 (top left), 13 (left), 19 (bottom left), 27 (bottom right), 101; **The White Company** p. 13 (right), 36 (bottom right), 42, 64, 81, 94, 98 (right), 141, 146 (left), 151 (bottom).

Useful Contacts

Karl Anderson & Soner
Rosendalagatan 6
561 22
Huskvarna
Sweden
www.karl-andersson.se

Laura Ashley
PO Box 19
Newton
Powys
SY6 1DZ
United Kingdom
www.lauraashley.com

Bsweden
Herråkra
Lenhovda
Sweden
www.bsweden.com

Davuka GRP Ltd
Unit 2c
The Wend
Coulsdon
Surrey
CR5 2AX
United Kingdom
www.decorative-coving.co.uk

Farrow & Ball
Uddens Estate
Wimbourne
Dorset
BH21 7NL
United Kingdom
www.farrow-ball.com

G.A.D.
Sodra Kyrkogatan 16
62156 Visby
Sweden
www.gad.com

Gustavian
19 New Quebec Street
London
W1H 7RY
United Kingdom
www.gustavian.com

Iform
Sundspromenaden 27
Box 5055
20071
Malmo
Sweden
www.iform.net

Marston & Langinger
192 Ebury Street
London
SW1W 8UP
United Kingdom
Tel: +44 (0)845 270 6688
www.marston-and-langinger.com

Nordic Style
Unit GF2
2 Michael Road
London
SW6 2AD
United Kingdom
www.nordicstyle.biz

Sprossa
Strandgata 9
4790
Lillesand
Norway
www.sprossa.no

Svenskt Tenn AB
Box 5478
11 84
Stockholm
Sweden
www.svenskttenn.se

Toast
D Ashmount Park
Upper Forest Way
Llansamlet
Swansea
SA6 8QR
United Kingdom
www.toast.co.uk

The White Company
Unit 30
Perivale Industrial Park
Horsenden Lane South
Greenford
Middlesex
UB6 7RJ
United Kingdom
www.thewhitecompany.com

Acknowledgements

Jeannine McAndrew and GMC Publications would also like to thank the following firms for their help:

Cole & Son (Wallpapers) Ltd
Lifford House
199 Eade Rd
London N4 1DN
Tel: +44 (0)20 8442 8844
www.cole-and-son.com

CW Textiles Ltd
The Courtyard
Royd Ings Avenue
Keighley
West Yorkshire BD21 4BZ
Tel: +44 (0)1535 617 300
www.coloroll.co.uk

Dulux
Dulux Customer Care Centre
ICI Paints
Wexham Road
Slough SL2 5DS
www.dulux.co.uk

Dunelm Mill
Dunelm (Soft Furnishings) Plc,
Fosse Way,
Syston,
Leicester LE7 1NF
Tel: +44 (0)8451 656 565
www.dunelm-mill.com

Francesca's Paints Ltd
34 Battersea Business Centre
99/109 Lavender Hill,
London SW11 SQL
Tel: +44 (0)20 7228 7694
www.francescaspaint.com

LG Harris & Co Ltd
Stoke Prior
Bromsgrove
Worcestershire B61 4AE
www.lgharris.co.uk

Hillarys
Colwick Business Park,
Private Road No 2,
Colwick,
Nottinghamshire NG4 2JR
Tel: +44 (0)800 916 6524
www.hillarys.co.uk

International Paints
Akzo Nobel Decorative Coatings
Crown House
Hollins Road
Darwen BB3 0BG
Tel: +44 (0)844 7709444
www.international-paints.co.uk

KA International
736 Fulham Rd
London SW6 5HD
Tel: +44 (0)20 7 736 5008
www.ka-international.com

Little Greene Paint Company
The Little Greene Paint Company
Limited
Wood Street
Openshaw
Manchester M11 2FB
Tel: +44 (0)161 230 0880
www.thelittlegreene.com

The Painted Curtain Pole Company
Unit 2, Springfield Farm
Perrotts Brook
Cirencester
Gloucestershire GL7 7DT
Tel: +44 (0)1285 831 771
www.thepaintedcurtainpole company.com

Richard Burbidge Mouldings
Whittington Road
Oswestry
Shropshire SY11 1HZ
Tel: +44 (0)1691 655 131
www.richardburbidge.co.uk

Robinson & Cornish Kitchens
St George's House
St George's Road
Barnstaple
Devon EX32 7AS
Tel: +44 (0)1271 329 300
www.robinsonandcornish.com

The Stencil Library
Stocksfield Hall
Stocksfield
Northumberland NE43 7TN
Tel: +44 (0)1661 844 844
www.stencil-library.com

Index

To place an order, or to request a catalogue, contact:
GMC Publications
Castle Place, 166 High Street, Lewes, East Sussex, BN7 1XU
United Kingdom
Tel: 01273 488005 Fax: 01273 402866
Website: www.gmcbooks.com
Orders by credit card are accepted